MW01032382

His Secret Garden Within You

His Secret Garden Within You

An Allegorical Journey to Wholeness

Emma Kelln
with devotions by Darien B. Cooper

DESTINY IMAGE® PUBLISHERS, INC.
P.O. Box 310, Shippensburg, PA 17257-0310
"Promoting Inspired Lives."

This book and all other Destiny Image and Destiny Image Fiction books are available at Christian bookstores and distributors worldwide. For more information on foreign distributors, call 717-532-3040. Or reach us on the Internet: www.destinyimage.com

Photography by Anselmo Amaro of Ella Rae Raabe

ISBN 13: 978-0-7684-0750-1
ISBN 13 EBook: 978-0-7684-0751-8

For Worldwide Distribution, Printed in the U.S.A.
1 2 3 4 5 6 / 18 17 16 15

Dedicated to the Bride of Christ,
That her trauma may be healed;
Thereby presenting her to her
Bridegroom without spot or wrinkle.

Contents

Preface

My heart's desire for you in this journey is for God Himself to touch and heal your soul, your very being, and for Him to mold you into His perfect image. In this process He will reveal to you your restored, flourishing garden (or soul) so that you can then nurture others and help them grow and be fruitful. Second Corinthians 5:17 (MSG) says, "The old life is gone; a new life burgeons!" The meaning of burgeon is to send forth new growth as buds or branches, to bloom, and to grow rapidly. Together we can fill the whole earth with the knowledge of God!

I am so honored that Darien Cooper has joined this second edition of my first book titled, *The Garden Within*, with her amazing devotional, creating this new book titled, *His Secret Garden Within You*. Her insight into the heart of God and her wisdom make this book a great tool for leading precious lives into wholeness and purpose. I am so grateful to God for bringing her into my life. As you journey through these pages, I believe you will begin to see yourself the way the Lord sees you, for He alone has the ability to heal your heart and soul of all lies, hurt, and pain. It is our desire for every reader to be touched and changed by God's love, which will in turn bring freedom and wholeness into your life so that you might do the same for others.

This journey of seeing my heart as His garden began for me many years ago. When God took my hand that day, He truly captured my heart. He took all of my insecurities, my hurt, and my pains as He walked and talked with me in the secret place—the garden within my soul. It was there, with Him, that I was healed. The Bible says in First Corinthians 3:9 that we are God's garden and vineyard under cultivation. To help you understand the state of my heart or my garden at the beginning of my journey, I need to share with you a very difficult time in my life that began me writing *His Secret Garden Within You*. I was a woman who by outward appearances seemed joyful and doing pretty much okay, but on the inside I was barren, insecure, and had very little of what God calls "the abundant life." I was more like the woman in Isaiah 54 who was forsaken and grieved and heart sore, broken hearted, because my now ex-husband not only had multiple affairs, but had also sexually abused my daughter (his stepdaughter) from the time she was 8 years of age until she was 12. It was after the fact that I found out. I have since learned that one in three girls is sexually abused and many never tell. Those statistics are heart wrenching!

There are a few great ministries to help victims, young and old, and also teach parents how to talk to their children about this violation in our world. Two I recommend: Voice Today (www.voicetoday.org) and Speaking Out Against Child Sexual Abuse (http://speakingout-csa.com). I personally have partnered with another great ministry that teaches about prevention and intervention for the sexually abused and also rescues individuals from sex trafficking: Life for the Innocent at http://lifefortheinnocent.org.

After seeking the Lord during this season, there was no fruit of repentance in my ex's life for the great devastation that he caused, and we were divorced. I moved out and the healing began. God Himself took me to the garden within my heart, into my soul, and it was there in the secret place that He took my pain and carried it Himself. He bound up my broken heart for my daughter, although it is still very painful if thought upon, and He promised me there, in the garden, that He would also heal her heart and cause her to flourish, which I have witnessed. For what the enemy meant to harm us and utterly destroy us, God has and will use that very thing to help others to find *wholeness* and *freedom* in Him as we share our lives with Him and for Him.

The vision or mission statement God gave me for *His Secret Garden Within You* is this: Jesus has taken every hurtful thing in my life and turned it into nourishment. This has caused me to grow into the person He created me to be, to nourish others, and to help them grow.

My prayer is that this journey will do the same for you.

IMPORTANT MESSAGE FOR MALE READERS: Although this book seems to be written for women, the truths are genderless and have already helped many men. Remember, men are also called the "Bride of Christ."

His Secret Garden Within You is an allegory. It refers to the study of elements, such as the earth or, in this case, gardens, as a structure or style used in writing. This one portrays a life change within a soul while one walks with Jesus through it. It is also the art of effective expression and the persuasive use of language that portray communication and discourse. In this writing, the allegorical form is conversations with Jesus in a garden setting. God uses analogies or parables throughout the Bible about gardens, often likening our lives to one. The allegory style is writing that is movingly expressive.

God, Jesus, the Master Gardener, absolutely knows what you and I were born for, because He created us for that purpose. He is perfecting us to be in His image. Before we were ever born, He knew us! He walked and talked with us in the very same garden you will enter on this journey. Will you let God, the Pruner and Gardener of your life, fashion you into His very image?

> *...You are God's garden and vineyard and*
> *field under cultivation...* (1 Corinthians 3:9).
> *"Here on this ground which is hard now,*
> *I will make it a vineyard."*
> *Love, Jesus*

I pray that this book will open your imagination to the Gardener's hand—God Himself working in and tending to the garden within your soul and your heart. I pray that He will give you an accurate description and vivid pictures of the condition of your heart (with and without Him) and the state of the garden that is within you. And I pray He will then release to you insights into your own story and the transformation of that story, scripted by your Master Gardener.

Let's enter in.

Picture this in your mind: a little girl walking in a vast garden setting. There are many walled gardens surrounding her, representing the people in her life that surround her every day. She walks around admiring the beauty in which she is enveloped. So many shades of color fill her eyes in the flourishing flowers that encircle her. The petals display brilliant purples, magnificent blues, bright yellows, and dashing whites, and in the leaves that climb up these garden walls are all the hues of green. Oh, the splendor of this place! She has entered into the setting of this story.

Now picture this little girl is you. It is not that you are necessarily young, but she is that precious little child inside each and every one of us—innocent, trusting, and searching. That little girl who longs to dance again, skip, twirl, and be free! She longs to be whole! The woman in this story is named Ally. Join me now as we enter the garden within her as she sees a sparrow fly by as if asking her to follow him. Here is where we begin.

Here is your story.

Emma Kelln

Introduction

What an awesome God we serve. He loves to be our wall of protection while He builds His Garden of Eden on earth from within us. He links His family together to be the rebuilder of His walls. That is what He did with Emma and me. He moved upon her heart to email me. The rest is history and manifested in this book. Our spirits were linked together to combine the flow of living water coming from our inner garden to release a greater flow for our garden's restoration and for others.

Have you ever felt like the garden of your soul was desolate, disgraced, and unfit for use? Or without friends, or hope and lonely? Do you need to be fortified with strength and made secure with greater courage and endurance? That is the mission Emma and I are undertaking. We are standing on His Word in Ezekiel:

> *The desolate land shall be tilled, that which had laid desolate in the sight of all who passed by. And they shall say, This land that was desolate has become like the garden of Eden, and the waste and desolate and ruined cities are fortified and inhabited. ...I the Lord have rebuilt the ruined places and replanted that which was desolate, I the Lord have spoken it, and I will do it* (Ezekiel 36:34-36).

As we journey together with our beloved Lord, our unmet needs, unhealed wounds, and unresolved issues begin to be solved as we learn to live in His presence knowing He is our safe place. We discover the only One who understands us perfectly, will never forsake us, always cares about us, who is glad to be with us, who hears us, listens to us, who empathizes with us, and who not only feels our pain but can also heal it. With Jesus as our inner companion we learn to enjoy being our true selves—humbly accepting and liking who we are. He shows us how to take back our land/garden and rebuild the desolate and ruined places. In this process our spirits, souls, and bodies are unified and replanted with His abundant life. This process takes time—it is time well spent!

Emma has written the allegory about Ally conversing with Jesus in the inner garden of her soul. The devotional guides take the same form. The conversational devotions represent questions many ask when desiring Jesus to enlighten our understanding. Jesus' responses are insights I have gained in my walk with Him. These truths have helped meet my inner needs, heal my wounds, and untangle unresolved issues. I trust they will be helpful to you as well. They are by no means considered infallible. Each devotional guide is similar to a capsule of meat that needs to be unpacked, developed, and custom designed to you personally. Each is a process that takes time to experience and clothe you with your particular aspect of His image. Hold them up to the Lord and ask Him to confirm what is for you and how to apply them to your own garden within. (The recommended readings at the end of the book are resources to help you unpack, develop, and research the topics I have simply touched upon.)

Each devotional builds upon the previous one. They are carefully designed to firmly establish you in Him and to strengthen your daily walk, so being in His presence becomes a way of life. The devotions are to be your journey guide in applying the truths to your individual journey. As you embrace the truths and apply them to your walk, they become yours experientially.

At the end of each chapter is a devotional guide inventory. These are for your individual use and can also be used in a small group study to guide your reflections and discussion. I suggest you keep a journal, writing down what God shows you—what pictures, images, or thoughts come to mind including those you are encouraged to write at the end of each devotional guide. Reading the Scriptures from different Bible translations can be helpful to glean a wider understanding and application.

With excitement, Emma and I welcome you into a journey with us that the garden of our souls be transformed into His Garden of Eden bringing His Kingdom to earth thereby releasing His glory.

Darien B. Cooper

CHAPTER 1

The Garden

Behold, He Comes

Ally was outside in her yard, working in her garden, when she saw a little sparrow fly by as if beckoning her to follow him. She took off her gardening gloves and walked toward her new feathered friend.

"What's over there?" Ally asked.

Suddenly she found herself before a great garden wall. Ally could only tell it was a wall because of its massive height. It stood straight up to the sky and reached as far as she could see horizontally. It was one of the most amazing sights she had ever seen. The wall was covered in ivy and decorated with brilliant purple clematis; climbing roses with petals of white, pink, and lavender; and pale, creamy honeysuckle, which seemed to be dancing in her sight.

"It's a garden," chirped the bird.

"Where's the door to get inside?" Ally asked.

It was then He approached her, the most captivating man she had ever seen in her life. He had wavy, shoulder-length hair, and He walked toward her with strength and majesty. The love that came from His eyes as He came near pierced her heart; just looking at His smile, she realized that she was accepted, loved, and adored. She knew in her heart who He was, that this was her beloved, her Jesus.

"I am the door!" He exclaimed.

He is speaking to *me*, she thought, standing in awe of Him. The words that came from His mouth were sweeter to her than anything she had ever tasted and more aromatic than any fragrance she had ever smelled.

She responded, "Your words are like honey to my soul. I feel them reach into my mind, my heart, and my emotions; they bring such sweetness to me."

"Your soul," He said, "that's where I am taking you, through this door. I am the door into the garden of your soul."

Ally looked at Him, a bit perplexed.

"You are a garden enclosed, and I call you My promised Bride." He held out His hand to her. "Rise up, My love, My fair one, and come away with Me into the secret safe place, into the garden within you."

DEVOTIONAL GUIDE 1

(The Devotional Guides are inserted periodically in the allegory to give you the opportunity to have your own journey to wholeness. As Ally converses with Jesus, Darien is conversing with Jesus not only representing questions with which many wrestle, but also relating them to Ally's journey. Hopefully, you, the reader, can identify, receive, and embrace the conversation as your own.)

"Jesus, I am glad for the sweetness Ally experienced, but my heart cries out for purpose. Why am I alive? How are the deep longings within satisfied? For what am I searching that I can't seem to find? Nothing works!

In my anguished, desperate cry, something began to move in the garden of my thirsty soul. Jesus was stirring the place He had planted deep within me to know Him who is the door to the abundant life for which I was seeking. He was drawing me to take the place in His heart that only I could fulfill.

Everything within me wanted to say, "Yes," but there were so many unanswered questions.

Jesus knew my thoughts, my apprehension, my wounds and fears. He said, *"Are you tired? Worn out? Burned out on religion? Come to me. Get away with me and you'll recover your life. I'll show you how to take a real rest. Walk with Me and work with me—watch how I do it. Learn the unforced rhythms of grace. I won't lay anything heavy or ill-fitting on you. Keep company with me and you'll learn to live freely and lightly"* (Matthew 11:28-30 (MSG)).

With all my strength, I said, "Yes."

With a beaming smile, Jesus said, "We will share this journey of the restoration of the garden of your soul together. There is no greater adventure you can experience. This adventure will take you beyond your greatest dreams, desires, thoughts, or hope. You will get to know Me, the King of kings and Lord of lords as your friend. You will get to know who you are in Me and enjoy being yourself. Such an adventure with Me is the best of the best!"

(I suggest you start your own journey to wholeness by keeping a journal. Write your response, insights, and longings after each Devotional Guide. Start now by reading and meditating upon Matthew 11:28-30 from different translations. Write down your inner desires, your feelings and your hopes. Please use the space below titled My Garden Within, to record what you are thinking and feeling as well as in your journal.)

My Garden Within

_____

_____

_____

"Please," Ally said, "do not look at me, and do not take me in there. I am afraid that I have taken care of and kept other gardens, but my own garden I have not cared for or kept."

He looked deeply into her eyes and spoke with more care and compassion than she had ever heard before.

He said, "Before you were ever born, I knew you and cared for you. I walked and talked with you in this very garden, through this door."

He pointed to Himself, yet she could see the enormous door He was about to push open with His mighty right hand.

"This garden was alive, awake, and flourishing; it was full of Me," Jesus proclaimed.

He smiled because He knew her, and He knew He was the author and finisher of her story. He had already seen her garden in its fullest state. He opened the door. They entered, and Ally's heart sank. It looked to be dead.

Oh Lord, it's too late; it's gone, she thought. For all she could see were brown, ugly masses of twisted branches, dead flowers, and fruitless trees. She thought about how her own garden at her home looked after the winter had taken its toll.

He seemed to have read her mind, for the next words that came from His mouth were, "I would know." He seemed to look right through her.

"Know what?" she asked sheepishly.

"I would know if it is dead or alive."

He then took out a small sword and grabbed a little branch that was lying motionless on the ground of her heart. When He cut off a sliver of it, Ally gasped. She felt it in her innermost being, because He had actually touched her very soul.

"The wick," He said, with a smile. "Do you see it?" He held the branch out toward her, saying, "It's green! This garden is not dead; it is as alive as you and Me."

DEVOTIONAL GUIDE 2

"I don't understand Jesus; You said there was a place only I could fulfill. How can I fill anything when my garden within is so troubled? That doesn't make sense to me. I don't feel I have anything to offer anyone especially You, the Creator of heaven and earth."

Jesus' response was tender as He always is when He said, "My precious, special one, before the foundation of the world I planned for you to be My chosen one who could release to the world part of Me that no one else could do. You were especially chosen to reflect a facet of my character and glory no one else can. I see that you are not dead, but in Me you become alive."

"How does this come about, Jesus?"

Jesus explained, "Enter into an intimate relationship with Me where we walk together, we talk together, and we get to know each other intimately. In this garden walk, tending to the things that interest you and Me, you will learn I am the One for whom you have been seeking. You will begin to grasp the love I have for you that fills heaven and earth and the heart of God."

He continued, "Listen to My Word, which is Me written down: *'Long before God our Father laid down earth's foundations, He had us in mind, had settled on us as the focus of His love to be made whole and holy by His love'"* (Ephesians 1:4 MSG).

"I am going to meditate on all this that is so new to me. Thank You for helping me grasp all You are saying."

(Carefully read and re-read Ephesians 1:4 from different translations. After a time of meditation, what is your heart saying? Make notes in your journal so you can remember and ponder truths revealed to you.)

My Garden Within

_____

_____

_____

Can this really be happening? Ally thought. *Is it possible that it is not too late—that He could still bring change and life to what looks and feels dead and lost?*

He interrupted her thoughts. "It is time, Ally," He said.

She looked up at Him. While gazing deeply into His eyes, she saw her own reflection and was taken aback by her love and affection for this man.

As she was being held by His eyes, she repeated, "Time," after realizing she had drifted away in His love for a moment.

"Do you want to stay this way?" He asked.

She held her breath, and He knew her answer.

"Then come away with Me, My beloved, for the winter is past, the rain is over and gone, the flowers appear on the earth, and the time of spring has come. Rise up."

He gently held out His right hand, and Ally took hold. At that moment He grabbed her very heart.

"I'll never, ever let you go," He said tenderly to her soul.

DEVOTIONAL GUIDE 3

Jesus, knowing I needed reassurance, said, "Once upon a time when there was no time, on the corner of nowhere where there was nothing, there was a meeting. The three of Us, Father, Myself His Son, and the Holy Spirit talked about how We loved loving each other. We wanted to expand Our family. We wanted to make you Our next of kin—to adopt you as Father's daughters and sons and for you to become My Bride. The Holy Spirit agreed and said He would reveal the Father's plan and My provision so that Our love could restore God's family garden of love within you and then this love could be released upon the earth."

Jesus confirmed His words with His written Word: *"Long, long ago he decided to adopt us into his family through Jesus Christ. (What pleasure he took in planning this!) He wanted us to enter into the celebration of His lavish gift-giving by the hand of his beloved Son"* (Ephesians 1:5-6 MSG).

Jesus challenged me, "Go outside and observe My creation in a flower blooming in your flower garden. This is something tangible you can see.

Marvel at My creative power, the beauty with which I create. As you release praise to Me, I will take the green wick within the seemingly dead parts of your garden and bring life into these places. I will do the inner work of transformation if you will do your part of cooperation. I want a partner. Will you do your part in this intimate relationship by talking and walking with Me in this way?"

My heart leaped. I knew this was what I was created for. I said, "Yes, Jesus, I will cooperate."

(Ponder Ephesians 1:5-6 and write down your response. Review what you see until it is established in you.)

My Garden Within

_____

_____

_____

The Healing Begins

She went with Him. They ascended first some rocky steps, going up a hillside, it seemed. Her Beloved said to her, "Oh, My Ally, while you are here in the seclusion of these rocks in your garden, in this secret and sheltered place with and in Me, let Me see your face, and let Me hear your voice. For your voice is sweet, and your face is so lovely to Me."

Ally was walking with her head hanging down, ashamed of the mess she had allowed her garden to become. Jesus stopped her, put His hand under her chin, and lifted her head. They were face to face. Her heart was suddenly touched, and she began to fervently sing to Him an old song that she had loved but had forgotten all about because of the difficult circumstances in her life.

She sang, and the song came from deep within. The words weren't just coming from her mouth, but from her heart as she sang with deep emotion and with all of her heart. All she wanted to do at that moment was to worship Him, because there they were, face to face in the garden of her soul. He was looking attentively into her eyes and into her soul.

She was loved by God Himself, and at that moment she knew it. At the same time, her thoughts were churning. She had been so consumed with her circumstances that she had ceased worshipping the lover of her soul.

I'm so sorry, Jesus; forgive me, Ally thought. She knew by the look on His face that He heard every one of her thoughts.

Everything around them appeared to be dead, yet Ally felt a little life, a little hope, and a little sun. She glanced at the ground and saw one tiny green shoot coming up; it was only about an inch tall. It was almost covered up with weeds. She bent down and pulled the weeds away from the tiny little plant.

"How did you know to pull the weeds?" Jesus asked.

She replied with a grin, "They were making it so the plant couldn't breathe."

Life.

He had begun gardening in her soul.

DEVOTIONAL GUIDE 4

"I have made such a mess of my life, Jesus, I am afraid to hope again. Every time I do, the hopes are dashed into a zillion pieces. I feel nothing but shame and guilt."

His voice comforted me once again through His Word and by quickening my soul, *"He has kept this secret for centuries and generations past, but now at last it has pleased him to tell it to those who love him and live for him, and the riches and glory of his plan are for you Gentiles, too. And this is the secret: that **Christ in your hearts is your only hope of glory"*** (Colossians 1:26-27 The Living Bible).

Jesus tenderly spoke to me saying, "Because you have given your heart to Me, I will rescue you from the shame, wounds, and lies the enemy has sought to use to destroy you. As we walk together, the healing will begin. I will bring you to wholeness." Then He added,

"With men this is impossible, but all things are possible with God" (Matthew 19:26).

"Jesus, I give to You all the places in my garden. Please bring forth the green shoots of life that I am not aware are even present in all the dead places I see."

(Thank Jesus, for He has begun the restoration of the garden in your soul. Memorize Colossians 1:26-27 and let it sink deeply within your soul. Write down your desires and hopes.)

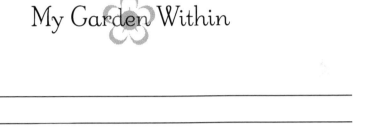

My Garden Within

Devotional Guide Inventory Chapter 1

1. Has your heart been searching for answers to life's questions? Have you been saying that you do not want to live life, or feel like you have been missing out on true life? Have you felt like you have never really had an abundant life?

2. Are you willing to let Jesus help you recover your life or restore the garden of your soul? Does it sound inviting to learn from the One who is life how to live freely and without bondage?

3. Reflect upon what it means to be able to fulfill a place in His heart that no one else can fill.

4. Have you ever considered that it gives Jesus great pleasure to walk and talk with you as His companion? How does that affect you?

5. When did you give your heart to Him? If you have not, would you consider doing so now? You can receive Jesus as your Savior right now by a simple prayer: "Jesus, thank You for dying on the cross for me personally. Come into my heart and cleanse me of all my sins by Your shed blood. Make me the person You designed me to be. Show me how to let You change me from the inside out. Amen."

My Garden Within Inventory

_____
_____
_____
_____
_____
_____
_____
_____
_____
_____
_____
_____
_____
_____
_____
_____
_____
_____
_____
_____

CHAPTER 2

A Secret Process

He who dwells in the secret place of the Most High shall remain stable and fixed under the shadow of the Almighty [Whose power no foe can withstand] (Psalm 91:1).
There is a time for everything, and a season for every activity under the heavens (Ecclesiastes 3:1 NIV).

This is the secret place," He said softly. "Ally, our time together is a protected, safe place where My arms fend off all harm. This is a sacred secret process where My abundant life is released to you." He put out His finger toward a branch, and a butterfly gently landed on it. He smiled.

"To everything there is a season and a purpose. There is a time to keep silent and a time to speak. There are a lot of things in your heart and your garden that need My hand, My strength, and My presence to heal. This is your time right now. This is a time for you to heal." As He was speaking, He stepped past an overgrown bush. "There is also a time to plant and a time to pluck up what is planted."

Her eyes stayed locked on Him.

"Gardens start with planning," He said. "Let Me be the Gardener, the Planner, the Author and the Finisher of My garden of you."

He was walking along in her garden and looking at every part, pulling dry things off here, throwing aside a stone there. He bent down and lifted up some soil from the ground of her heart. He could not grab hold of very much, because the ground underneath was so hard.

Ally took a deep breath.

He went on, "Do you know what grows in uncultivated, hard ground? Only weeds. Where there is no seed, weeds grow, and weeds choke the life out of things. We will talk about weeds soon enough, though." He smiled playfully at her. "It is time, My Ally, to break up your uncultivated ground; this is your part, My beloved."

His eyes penetrated her very being; they seemed to look right into her soul and her emotions. With His eyes He grasped her inner significance, and she felt kept by Him, protected, and covered.

DEVOTIONAL GUIDE 5

"Good morning, Jesus. Thank You for showing me my heart was longing for intimacy with You while I tried to fill it in all the wrong places. As a result, the inner garden of my soul became dry and thirsty because I was not seeking to walk and talk with You. I didn't even know You wanted to walk with me. Now that I know, I want to go with You to the deep places in my soul, so that not only am I satisfied within, but also that Your glory, Your presence, would be released in and through me to others. Thank You for my destiny in You. Now I have a purpose. I have another question, how do I cooperate with You to break up my uncultivated, hard ground?"

"I am so glad you asked," Jesus responded. He answered by sharing words He had written a long time ago, *"The secret [of the sweet, satisfying companionship] of the Lord have they who fear (revere and worship) Him, and He will show them His covenant, and reveal to them its [deep, inner] meaning. My eyes are ever toward the Lord, for He will pluck my feet out of the net"* (Psalm 25:14-15).

Jesus continued, "Remember, My special one, those who fear Me (which is to revere and worship Me) are those who allow Me to be their very life, giving Me My rightful place in their lives. They fear getting out of our secret place, because they realize there and only there is life. To worship Me is to walk with Me in companionship. Learn to refocus your eyes on Me so I can pluck you out of the enemy's ways."

"Yes, Jesus, with Your help and strength I will walk in companionship with You, with my eyes focused upon You."

(Consider the thoughts presented. Read Psalm 25:14-15 and add Psalm 42:1-2, 7. Write down your response.)

My Gaden Within

_____

_____

_____

"Will you trust Me, Ally? Will you give up your plan and your heart and trust Me?"

She had been so consumed by her own painful circumstances that her self had begun to reign and had taken her heart captive. In her life Ally was only focusing her attention on the things that were temporal and had no lasting satisfaction to her soul or to her emotions. She did this to try to fill the void in her life and the emptiness she felt deep inside because of past wounds. The things of the world had grasped her gaze and captivated her thought life. She gave more time to them and to the negative happenings around her than to God.

Jesus continued, "Your part is to seek Me, to crave Me with your whole heart, as your soul's first necessity." He stopped and looked at Ally, right into her eyes, "In all the hurt, pain, and troubles of your soul, your mind, and your emotions, I will turn it around and use it all for My good."

Ally thought, *Could it be? Could He really make something out of my life, this mess of a garden that I see in front of me? Could He actually use me for Himself?* She smiled vaguely, wanting so badly to believe what Jesus was saying to her.

Jesus then picked up a dead branch He had stepped on and broke it in two.

"With what that old serpent, satan, meant to use to harm you and bring you to total destruction, I will use for good, to magnify Myself in your life and in the lives of others. I will use it for the purpose of showcasing you, My trophy of grace. You will show forth My presence and the result of that presence within and around you to all with whom you come into contact by My divine appointments, and you will pour forth My love to the world. I will make Myself known through you to a lost and dying world."

DEVOTIONAL GUIDE 6

"My heart is in awe, Jesus, that You want to showcase me to be Your trophy of grace. Can You really turn around all the hurt, pain, and troubles of my soul and heal my emotions using it for good? Help me to understand and to receive Your grace. Show me the way."

Jesus was delighted to share. "It is in My presence where fullness of joy is experienced. Your part is to cooperate with Me by staying in My presence. You do that by conversing with Me, relying upon Me and letting Me be your inner companion. Talk to Me as if you could see and feel Me. You are used to getting your identity by attempting to please others, to promote or hide yourself. Instead, as you re-direct your attention to Me, an audience of One, you will discover who I created you to be and you will delight in yourself as I always delight in you."

He then added, "My love, when you are tempted, either out of habit or unsurrendered desires, to monitor your awareness or actions by another, you are walking in their presence not Mine. Without realizing it, you are trying to get another's approval or favor rather than enjoying companionship with Me. By doing so, you leave My presence and enter into another's presence. Turn back to Me knowing I am glad to be with you. Others may not be, but I always am. I never moved from you, nor will I ever."

With much compassion Jesus added, "Be patient with yourself. These truths are learned one step at a time. It is a gradual process that is worth the patience it requires to be whole."

"Jesus, all this is so new to me. I love learning about how to really live the abundant life with You."

(As you bask in these truths, quietly meditate upon Psalm 16:5-11 with special emphasis on verse 11. Jot down your thoughts.)

My Garden Within

_____

_____

_____

He looked at the ground. "Here on this ground, which is hard now, I will give you vineyards. I will transform the valley of trouble into a door of hope and expectation for you. This garden within you will blossom and send forth shoots, and it will fill the whole world with the fruit of knowing Me, the one true God. What that means is that you will share your story, Ally, and people will come to Me. And you will sing here again, Ally, and you will dance and twirl, as in the days of your youth. You will feed many with the fruits that will grow here, and many gardens will flourish as you walk by them. People will change because of this life in you—because of My life in you."

The sun was setting. The sky turned a rich salmon color, and the night air began to take on a slight chill.

Her beloved Jesus began to sing:

> *I have come into My garden, My promised Bride.*
> *You, oh enemy, and you, distractions of the world,*
> *You can never make My lover disloyal to Me.*
> *She is Mine. Drink, yes, drink abundantly of love,*
> *Oh precious one, for now I know you are Mine.*

He sang this song as a proclamation over her life. With His confident words still thrilling her heart, her beloved Jesus turned, and His physical presence disappeared into the night.

Ally then found herself once again at her little house. She went to sleep that night, but her heart stayed awake; she dreamt that she heard the voice of her Beloved.

DEVOTIONAL GUIDE 7

"Good night, Jesus. You have done well by me today. Thank You! As I am learning to focus on You being my inner companion, working in the garden of my soul, help me to understand the difference between being with You and doing for You. Am I called a human being for a reason and not a human doer? Am I really lovely to You because of who I am and not what I do for You?"

Jesus smiled with excitement. He said, "All My loved ones struggle with this one. When they try to perform to win My delight they fail. When they stay in My presence fellowshipping with Me, we do together what is on My heart and your real heart. They, therefore, live supernaturally. Listen to My words in Hebrews: *"Let us therefore be zealous and exert ourselves and strive diligently to enter into that rest [of God, to know and experience it for ourselves], that no one may fall or perish by the same kind of unbelief and disobedience [into which those in the wilderness fell]"* (Hebrews 4:11).

"I need only your assent and cooperation, My precious one, to stay in My presence. When you move away from Me, the Holy Spirit will make you aware you are attempting to perform rather than cooperate with Me. He is your Helper."

"Jesus, this helps. I will deliberately turn to You, trusting and enjoying Your presence."

(Soak in the following verses: Hebrews 4:11 and John 14:26-28; 16:7-14. What comes to your mind? Write it down.)

My Garden Within

_____

_____

_____

Devotional Guide Inventory Chapter 2

1. What are the things in life that you thought would fulfill you and give you life? Did it work on a deep, permanent level? How long did it take to realize this wasn't the answer?

2. Where do you find fullness of joy that gives pleasure to you and to Jesus according to Psalm 16:11? How does this change the way you live? How do you feel about this truth?

3. Where are we to be living as a way of life? How can we tell when we are not in His presence? What is the difference between *being* in Him and *doing* for Him?

My Garden Within Inventory

_____

_____

_____

_____

_____

_____

_____

_____

_____

_____

_____

_____

_____

_____

_____

_____

_____

_____

_____

_____

_____

CHAPTER 3

Awakened

"For I know the plans I have for you," declares the Lord, "plans to prosper you and not to harm you, plans to give you hope and a future" (Jeremiah 29:11 NIV).

Ally awoke hearing a song in her heart. She knew the voice. It was Jesus, and once again He was singing:

> *Come away My beloved. Come away My beloved.*
> *Come away My beloved, to our place I'm calling you.*
> *Come away My beloved. Come away My beloved.*
> *Come away My beloved.*
> *I long to be with You.*

She again entered into the garden of her soul and found that Jesus had been working, even while she was sleeping. She felt a bit brighter as she looked around; things began to turn a little greener right before her very eyes. These words came to Ally's heart: Yield. Surrender. Give up something. Everything.

"Lord, I want You to be my Gardener," she prayed. "Have Your way, and make my soul a beautiful place where You would like to be with me. Direct my paths; direct where I go and when I go there. I just ask that You hold me during this process," she paused for a moment, "and I just want to add that I trust You." His voice was becoming clearer as she chose to stay in the secret place, her garden. She then felt His arms surrounding her. He held her close. Her eyes welled up with tears. She felt so safe and so cherished.

"Are you ready?" He asked, continuing to hold her.

She wasn't quite sure what He meant by that, but she responded before her mind could take her away.

"I'm so ready," she replied. "I cannot remain in the state I am in. I heard these words this morning when I awoke and came here to our garden— that I must surrender, yield, give up something, everything. I surrender, Jesus, to Your perfect plan and will for my life."

She took a deep breath and said, "I seek You, Lord, with all that I am and hope to become."

DEVOTIONAL GUIDE 8

"Thank You, Jesus, for warming my heart with Your presence, helping me begin to feel safe. I do not want to miss anything You are saying to me. How can I be sure I hear Your voice? There have been so many voices in my life saying different things. I want to know the truth and be surrendered to You."

Jesus was so delighted to answer. "Precious one, Ally heard My voice when the song came to her heart this morning and once again when the thought to surrender entered her mind. I often speak in such ways. I said when I was on earth that *"My sheep listen to my voice; I know them, and they follow me"* (John 10:27 NIV). Notice it is a process of moving from being a lamb to a sheep. You heard My voice when you, as a lamb, invited Me to be your Savior. As you mature, becoming a sheep, you will discover the many ways in which I speak to you."

Jesus continued, "I speak in many different ways. One is through creation to show you My creativity, power, and love. Sometimes I bring a thought across your mind that you know is good and different from what you think. With this thought is a *knowing* that it is Me. Other times you have an impression, maybe to call someone or to pray for them. You may feel a tug or an explosion in your heart when you are reading

My Word. The written Word suddenly makes sense. I also communicate though dreams, visions, trances, others' words, or occasionally an audible voice. But mostly it is a still, small inner voice. However, My voice never contradicts My written Word. It is also good to check with others who are walking closely with Me. They can help you separate My voice from destructive voices."

"Jesus, I'm excited about learning to live with You in a whole new way than I have ever lived before. Thank You for loving me so much."

(Read John 10:1-5, 27; Isaiah 30:21; and Deuteronomy 13:4. What speaks to your heart? Write your insights down and review them.)

My Garden Within

_____

_____

_____

Her words touched His heart. She could feel His very heartbeat because He held her close. She remained so still, and she did not want Him to ever let go. She listened with her spirit in the silence of the moment, wanting so badly to feel accepted and loved by Him and to truly receive the great love that He had for her. She began to feel the pain in her heart again from the one in her life who had been unfaithful to her, had wounded her heart, and made the ground of that same heart very hard and untrusting. Then she turned her focus back to the only One she knew could truly heal that pain.

Jesus whispered in her ear, "Can I keep you?"

She turned and looked Him straight in the eyes. "I am Yours," she replied, smiling, tears running down her hopeful face.

He took His hands and held her face gently up to look upon His. He would not allow her to look down.

"I love you," He said, looking right into her big brown eyes as she began to weep.

He again spoke, saying, "I love you."

She looked into His eyes and saw her own reflection once again. She thought, *His voice and speech are exceedingly sweet. Yes, He is altogether lovely. The whole of Him delights and is precious. This is my Beloved, and this is my Friend. Keep speaking, for my heart longs to hear Your voice.*

He again spoke, saying, "You are beautiful, My love. Behold, you are beautiful. You have dove's eyes, and dove's eyes can only see right in front of them, as they are focused. Keep your eyes, My love, on Me. Look not to the things of this world to satisfy you. Look to Me. Gaze at Me. Only I can satisfy the longing of your heart."

He gently kissed her forehead. And they began again to walk in her garden.

 DEVOTIONAL GUIDE 9

"I love learning to be with You, Jesus. I am just beginning to see that walking in Your presence as my inner companion is bringing comfort to my broken heart. Please tell me how this works as I learn to hear Your voice and embrace this new journey."

Jesus said with tender excitement, "This is a mystery I love to share with you, My special one. When I left earth having finished the work Father gave Me to do, providing all you need to become whole, I sent the Holy Spirit to live in those who received Me as their Savior. You actually became My dwelling place here on earth. Isn't that amazing?"

"Jesus, I am not good enough for You to live within me. Help me to understand how this could happen."

Jesus gently stroked and lifted my fallen face and said, "Remember, My love, I am the One who makes all things pure, holy, and righteous. When we walk together, My light covers all the dark things that have been done, will be done, and the things you have done. I enable you to live from the new heart I gave you when I came to live inside as your

Savior. As we walk together, we will deal with the dark things one at a time under My gentle loving care. You have nothing to fear. Relax and get to know My loving heart for you."

"Jesus, I'm excited about discovering this mystery with You as we walk together."

(Spend some time letting this sink deeply into your inner being, My precious one. Use My words to give you insight from 1 Corinthians 3:16; 1 John 1:7; and 2 Corinthians 5:17. Write down your thoughts, questions, and insights.)

My Garden Within

_____

_____

_____

Purpose and Planning

"The purpose of a garden is to enrich the quality of life on the land that is under your control," He said. "Is that not why you have your flower and vegetable garden, Ally?"

She nodded, just wanting to soak in every word being spoken by Him. His words spoke right into her heart.

He continued, "You are My garden, My promised Bride. I have come into this garden to give you life and to enrich your quality of life."

He smiled because He knew He was able.

"Your garden can be beautiful by choice, letting Me, the Gardener, do My job, or it can remain dead, ugly, and unchanged."

She thought to herself, *You can feel really ugly on the inside even though the outside may look pretty good. Oh, I long to be whole.*

Jesus continued, "My Father always told Me to make use of all the potential land…and you have potential. Why? Because you have the Holy Spirit within you—My Father's very Spirit, My very Spirit, living inside you.

When you asked Us to come into your life, We came. We came for this land."

He stomped His foot on the ground and said, "There is no such thing as useless land. You are valuable."

Ally found that hard to believe, but His eyes, looking into hers, spoke the truth.

"Now let's see what we have to work with."

He looked over the entire garden of her soul and just smiled.

"The Gardener brings the change," He said.

She considered that statement for a moment, thinking, *Does my garden have a choice when I go out to work on it? Does it say, "No, don't take that away!" No, it just yields, surrenders, gives up, and submits.* There were the words again that she had heard that morning. *Oh, help my unyielding heart!*

⊱ DEVOTIONAL GUIDE 10 ⊰

"Jesus, my heart is shaky, but You have given me a breath of hope that things can be different. Please reassure me of my purpose and calling and that You have this all under control."

Jesus' eyes danced with delight because He had such good news for His beloved. "My love, remember the meeting I shared where Father, Holy Spirit, and I had you in mind when We chose you and planned your journey? Father's plan was to give you life and life abundantly. I agreed to come to earth to make provision for your life. The Holy Spirit is living within you to bring forth Father's plan and My provision. As you cooperate by walking with Me, listening to My voice, and choosing to use your will to obey, you not only find Me, but you also start taking back the ground the enemy stole from you.

"I am trustworthy and faithful My beloved. You can trust Me to bring this about. Your calling is to walk in companionship and participation with Me. My Word written by Paul in First Corinthians 1:9 describes this clearly: '...*you were called into companionship and participation with His Son, Jesus Christ our Lord.*' You are learning beautifully to enjoy walking in My presence, which is your calling. How I use you will become evident later as your godly passions are developed. I am so pleased with you."

"How exciting, Jesus, to know what my calling is. I will cooperate with You to bring my calling into full maturity."

(Carefully and prayerfully read John 10:10; Jeremiah 29:12-14a; 1 Corinthians 1:9; and 1 Thessalonians 5:24. Which verses mean the most to you? Write down your thoughts.)

My Garden Within

_____

_____

_____

She looked to Him again, and He was standing tall with confidence. With His vision expanding for her, He continued evaluating the existing plants.

"I plan to keep as many of the better specimens as possible," He said. "Established trees and mature shrubs become important components of the garden—those things that you have been taught by God already, that which is deeply rooted in you. These are established truths within you that have been developed by God—truths that are firm and unchanging, the godly plantings of our Father."

He paused as He watched a hummingbird flutter its wings right in front of Him, as if it were praising Him just for a moment.

Ally smiled.

He continued, "Before any irrevocable decisions are made, existing plants should be evaluated for their potential contributions in your garden."

He kept walking and looking at every little part of her soul. She followed Him ever so closely.

"Contributions of shade and resting places, leaves of healing, flowers in each of the four seasons of the soul, and a place of refuge from the storms of life. And we can't forget the beautiful blooms that give off a sweet smell when the day has been hard and you just need to get away to be with Me."

He turned to a rose bush in her garden, and it immediately produced a beautiful pink rose. He picked it, smelled it Himself, and handed it to Ally. She smiled at Him, and she too smelled its sweetness.

He climbed up a little wall that was built out of unhewn stones and looked over the whole of her.

"Some things that My Father has planted in your life, I will leave as a memorial of God's grace and goodness. Some of them were unpleasant to you, but they will bear fruit that you can feed others with because you have been through them."

He then gazed through Ally's countenance, into her heart. He said, "Those things in your life that crushed you and bruised your heart—I will take those very things and make them into bread to feed the multitudes."

He took her hand, and they began to walk again. A small breeze rustled the trees surrounding them; it was as if they were applauding. He then stopped at a bush that had become very overgrown, taking up so much room in her garden that it had begun to encroach upon the other plantings of the Lord. It had started to overstep the limits of what had belonged to, or was due to, Another.

"This definitely needs to be pruned. Ally, will you allow Me to move, remove, or prune some things in your garden? Things that could hurt you or give too much shade to the plants around them, thus causing them not to grow in the Son?"

Again, Ally trusted Jesus, responding, "I believe that You will do what is best for my life and my garden." She gazed down at her beautiful rose and then back to Him. "Lord, I choose to yield."

DEVOTIONAL GUIDE 11

"My precious one, I want you to know that because you have chosen to walk with Me, you are releasing an exquisite fragrance which is not only healing to you, but is drawing others to Me," Jesus shared.

"That seems impossible, my Lord. How can that be?"

Jesus smiled knowing this truth would set me free. He explained, "You cannot live the Christian life, only I can live the Christian life through you. As you are relying upon Me, My life flows in and through you, bringing healing within and flowing onto others so they can be drawn to walk with Me also. Isn't that good news?"

"Jesus, I have tried before to do the right thing, but I never could for very long. How is this different?"

Jesus held her gaze with such compassion. He said, "My beloved, I know you have tried. Now My resurrection power, which is the greatest power in heaven and earth, is available to you from within. I will strengthen your spirit; I will settle your troubled soul and uphold you with My righteous right hand. No foe can stop us! I defeated all foes on the cross."

"Yes, that is good news, Jesus! I am amazed at what You have provided for me."

(Meditate on the following Scriptures and write down what they mean to you. Read 2 Corinthians 2:14-15; Galatians 2:20; Ephesians 1:19-23; and Isaiah 41:10.)

My Garden Within

_____

_____

_____

He lifted her up and spun her around and laughed. He loved her submissive heart.

He set her down next to a handsome plant, and He spoke again, saying, "No matter how handsome a plant may be, if it is obviously in the wrong place, it should be moved or cut down. I will not hesitate to take out the shrubs or trees that are taking up so much room in your garden that they have begun to cast shadows so that you cannot see or enjoy more desirable plantings of the Lord."

Ally began to think of the things that had begun to take up so much time in her life. They weren't all necessarily bad things—she just gave too much time to them.

Jesus sat on a big stone in her garden and pulled Ally to His side. "Redeem your time, Ally, for the days can be taken over by evil. There is an enemy in this world that desires to steal your time away and to keep you distracted. You need to choose to set your mind on the things above and to stay balanced. If you don't spend time with the Gardener, He can't as effectively work on your garden."

Jesus stood up and walked over to a stately weed that had grown in pride, haughtiness, and self. The weed immediately bowed. "Will you allow Me to pull up these things?"

He bent down and grabbed the stately weed at its surface, where it had begun to grow in her.

"These are the strongholds planted in your life by bad choices or circumstances or mindsets. Can I pull them out to make room for the plantings of the Lord?"

"Yes," she replied. "With Your grace and wisdom, yes."

With her permission, He pulled up the weed. He had an expression of pleasure on His face and continued, saying, "My will is to restore you to your original form. Remember when I told you that before you were ever born I knew you? That I walked and talked with you in this very garden?"

Ally nodded.

Jesus, seeing her, said, "My plan is to return you to that state and that condition. I want to repair and renew your soul. I want to again take possession of you, My garden, My bride, My love. To restore all that was yours and all of the fruits of your field from the day you left the land even until now. I will also restore or replace for you the years that the locust has eaten, and you shall eat here and be satisfied. You shall feed many and praise the name of the Lord your God, who has dealt wondrously with you."

They sat down under an apple tree to rest for a while, and, as Ally looked up through the branches into the sky, she remembered a song. She sang it to herself as He listened with His heart.

> *Like an apple tree among the trees of the wood,*
> *So is my beloved among the sons!*
> *Under His shadow I delight to sit,*
> *And His fruit was sweet to my taste.*

She felt His left hand under her head, and His right hand embraced her. She drifted off to sleep in His incredible peace.

DEVOTIONAL GUIDE 12

"Jesus, there are so many thoughts and feelings swilling around in my head and heart. What is to be removed from the garden of my soul... how is it to be done and when will it all take place?"

As always, Jesus had an answer. "Precious one, I would like you to read words I spoke through David in the Twenty-third Psalm many years ago. These words comforted David, and I want you to be comforted by them also. It will give you an overall picture of My provision and how it will end well for you. As you read each verse, rely upon the Holy Spirit to open your eyes to see what I am saying to you. Say the verses over and over until they seep into your inner being, becoming yours. When troubling thoughts arise, speak the verse out loud that speaks to your situation. Start now."

"Yes, I will Jesus. I will say them over and over to myself until they are mine."

(Memorize Psalm 23. Make it personal by putting your name into each verse. Rest in what is being said, allowing your soul to be comforted and your spirit to be strengthened.)

My Garden Within

_____

_____

_____

Devotional Guide Inventory Chapter 3

1. When was the first time you realized that God wanted to speak to you? What did you feel He was saying to you? What are the ways in which He speaks? Which ones have you experienced? Why would God want to speak to His children?

2. Did you know that receiving Jesus as your Savior made you the dwelling place of the Holy Spirit? What difference does that make in the way we treat our bodies? How does this make you feel?

3. What is your calling or purpose in life according to First Corinthians 1:9? What is the provision made available to fulfill this calling or purpose in your life?

4. How is the Christian life lived? When He is living within you, what results will others as well as you become aware of?

5. Have you ever memorized Scripture? It is not that hard. Simply say it over and over to yourself until it is established in your mind. God wants to use memorized Scriptures to strengthen us, encourage us, and to increase brain power capacity. Jot down how God uses Scripture in your life.

My Garden Within Inventory

_____

_____

_____

_____

_____

_____

_____

_____

_____

_____

_____

_____

_____

_____

_____

_____

_____

_____

_____

_____

_____

_____

CHAPTER 4

Dark but Comely

Dark am I, yet lovely to Him (Song of Solomon 1:5).

As Ally slept, she had a dream. In her dream she saw herself before a great crowd of women at a conference, and she was speaking to them with compassion in her voice.

She said to them, "God wants you to lift your faces to Him so that He can give you His life. His desire is to touch and heal your soul, your very being. He longs to mold you into His perfect image. As you continue to look to Him, He will reveal to you your restored, flourishing garden. He wants to bring life to your soul so you can then nurture others and help them grow and be fruitful also."

She was so filled with Jesus Himself that He radiated out of her being. He began to touch the very desires in the heart of each woman standing before her; she knew this because they all began to weep.

She thought, *Deep within each of us is the longing to be a handmaiden for the Lord—to be filled and changed and to be an instrument of His love and peace to a hurting, challenged world.*

She began to speak to the women again. "He desires intimacy with you, and He told me that." She smiled. "So we are going on a journey to the garden of our souls; we are going to the secret place to be with Him, to spend time with Him, the lover and caretaker of our gardens. We are going to be recreated by the Master Gardener Himself. It is time to rise up and go with Him into this garden. This garden is within your hearts, because when you find God in your own hearts, you find Him everywhere."

Ally awoke from her dream, and she began to cry. She realized that it had reflected what Jesus had done in her own garden already and showed her that the truths He had taught her were for a purpose—and that was for her to teach others. She was alone now, in the garden of her soul.

Ally thought, *Oh, to be beautiful to the Lord, and for Him to touch others through me! But look at me,* she thought, *I am darkened by the things of this world, and some of the choices I have made. How could He ever use someone as dark as I am?*

DEVOTIONAL GUIDE 13

"Jesus, my heart begins to be encouraged as I choose to walk with You. My heart then shakes as I realize the ugliness within me that I simply have not been able to overcome. I don't want to lose what I have gained, but I need Your thoughts not mine."

Jesus responded with great passion. "My delightful one, I have eternal eyes. Remember, We knew you before the foundation of the world. You have Our DNA within you. You are made in Our image. We see your potential. We see the finished real you. I am not confined to time as you are."

Jesus continued, "I will quote My words I wrote many years ago. *'Let Us make man in Our image, according to Our likeness...God's nature abides in him—His principle of life, the Divine Seed, remains permanently within him.'* The Divine Seed is speaking of Me, and We were talking about you in these verses, delightful one," Jesus said as He gave me a warm, affectionate smile.

"Your focus, delightful one, is to continue to remember that I do the transforming or restoration in your soul as you fellowship with Me. I know what to touch, heal, and restore at the right time and the right place. Your part is to receive My words, allowing them to sink deeply into your heart so that the winds of wholeness have freedom to do Our work."

"It is so comforting, Jesus, to know what my part is. I am learning to trust You."

(Meditate on Genesis 1:26-27 and 1 John 3:8-10. The Amplified translation reveals these truths especially well in these verses. Ask the Holy Spirit to make His words real within as you not only read them but also ponder them in your heart during the day.)

My Gaden Within

_____

_____

_____

She fell to the ground with her face in the dirt and cried bitter tears of repentance for her past and for her lack of trust.

She began to ask herself these questions with tear-filled eyes: *Does my soul really crave the Master Gardener, even in the presence of the best the world can offer me? Do I have a constant sense of Jesus' presence with me and in me, regardless of what surrounds me? Do I take time to meet my Gardener each day, letting Him tend my soul? And do I take the time to let Him tell me of His love for me? Do I cheer His heart with my interest in Him, or do other things captivate my heart and life? Do I realize that my voice lifted in praise and song is sweet to Him, or do I withhold it?*[1]

Ally was conversing with her soul, asking herself these questions, and covering the soil beneath her face with tears. She was realizing who she was without Him and desiring to be transformed into His very image.

It was at that moment she began to hear the wind rustling the leaves above her and felt it blowing all around her. As she lifted her face from the soil, something beautiful happened. The wind seemed to compact right before her eyes. It swirled her tears with the dirt in the puddle before her and then lifted. She felt a soft breeze touch her cheeks as if a feather were brushing them lightly.

A bottle appeared before her, and the tears that were left on her cheeks gently fell into it. Then the wind and the bottle ceased to be. She glanced down at where her tears were mingled with the dirt and saw a shiny, little black stone. She picked it up and placed it close to her heart.

DEVOTIONAL GUIDE 14

"I identify with Ally. I need to repent of so much, Jesus. How do I repent? What if I cannot repent enough or correctly? This is all so new to me."

Jesus gently and tenderly leaned over His special one saying to her, "Repentance is simply changing direction from walking the wrong way to walking the right way. Repentance is a gift from God that I give to you. I give the ability to receive truth, and that truth then transforms your mind."

He went on to add, "Repentance comes from the Greek word *metanoia* and means 'to perceive afterward' or 'after thought' or 'to think again' or 'rethink.' As you allow My mind to become your mind, you will rethink your position in light of truth, or change your mind based on the fact that you thought wrongly before and need to embrace the truth about yourself. You are to be constantly adjusting your mind in light of new, truthful information.

"Special one that is a critical part of being transformed into My image. The change happens as We do the work in the garden of your soul. When you see how you have thought incorrectly about yourself, replace it with the truth and walk as if you felt it."

"Yes, this helps me know how to walk with You in repentance, cooperating in my transformation. This helps remove some of the mystery. Thank You so much."

(Meditate upon 1 Corinthians 2:16; Matthew 4:17; John 8:32; and Romans 2:4. Write down what speaks to your heart.)

My Garden Within

_____

_____

_____

She asked herself, *What could this mean?*

She lifted herself from her knees and turned to see Jesus.

He too had tear-filled eyes, and He told her the meaning of the little black stone. He said, "You are dark but beautiful to Me."

Ally held her breath as He continued, "Even in your weakness I see that your heart truly wants Me, and that is beautiful to Me. I desire your intimacy, your time, and your worship."

He wiped a tear from His face.

Ally realized He was crying tears for her. He so desired her companionship and her love that it brought His very heart to tears.

She thought, *He is crying for me.*

That thought grabbed her heart and changed it immediately.

He cleared His throat and continued, "The wind was My very Spirit working with your prayers and forming them into this reminder to yourself. This little stone you hold in your hand shall be a memorial for you. It is to remind you of what We have done for you this day—to remind you that though you are dark, you are truly beautiful to Us. That even in your unrefined state and in the process of being remade, We see you as beautiful—'We' meaning My Father, Me, and the Holy Spirit. We all have unconditional, extravagant love for you." Ally could not speak; she just received His words into her garden as she tightly grasped the tiny little stone.

"We are going to replant you, Ally. Your desolate land shall be tilled—land that has lain desolate in the sight of all who passed by and said of it, 'This life is unfit for use and without hope.' Those same people shall now say, 'This once desolate land and life have become like the Garden of Eden.' Then those around you, those who have known you before and your new acquaintances, shall know that I the Lord have rebuilt the ruined places in your heart. I have replanted that which was desolate. This is what I speak over you, Ally, and I will do it!"

Ally recalled her dream of speaking before thousands of women, knowing it had to be His hand that had even planted this dream inside her. She still was unable to speak and looked back into His eyes. She thought to herself, *Whether I speak before thousands or only to a few, this life change within me is not only for myself but for others also.*

DEVOTIONAL GUIDE 15

"Jesus, these words have been spoken to me, 'You are worthless. You will never amount to anything. You are but a worm for others to use or step upon.' I have believed it, Lord. Can my mind really be changed as I embrace Your words, Your truth, and walk in Your presence?"

With exuberant ecstasy Jesus answered, "My beloved, as you walk with Me in your everyday, ordinary life—your sleeping, eating, going-to-work, and walking-around life—embracing what I am doing for you is good, I will do the rest. As you fix your attention on Me, I will change you from the inside out. Listen to My voice and quickly respond to it. I will bring the best out of you, developing well-formed maturity and wholeness in you" (see Romans 12:1-2 MSG).

Jesus continued, "My precious one, you are no accident. We planned for you. As you turn your heart toward Me, you are face to face with Me. I, who am personally present, a living-Spirit, am setting you free of the ugly, untrue words spoken against you by others and by yourself. There is nothing between you and Me. Your life is gradually becoming brighter and more beautiful because I am entering your life and filling your garden, and you are becoming like Me. My process is amazing!"

"Jesus, You give me new hope. Thank You."

(Carefully read and ponder Romans 12:1-2 and 2 Corinthians 3:18 from different translations. Write down your thoughts.)

My Garden Within

_____

_____

_____

He reached into His pocket and pulled out a little black pouch.

He held it out to her and said, "Here, for your stone. Keep it with you as a memorial of the day when the Holy Spirit revealed your beauty in the process."

She took the pouch from His hand, placed the shiny black stone in it, and held it to her heart.

Jesus then threw His head back and laughed. He was so thrilled with her submissive, captivated heart that He grabbed her hand and began to run with her. They ran in her garden to a river that seemed to have appeared almost out of nowhere. It was beautiful and flowing with clean, untainted water. This river was in her, inside her garden.

He said, "This is our River of Life. We created it to flow in and out of you. In this life-giving river is the promise, and as you cross it you will receive everything you need for life and godliness. This is where the Holy Spirit retrieved the sediment that, combined with your tears, created your first stone of promise."

Ally reached down and put her hand in the life-giving river. As she did, again she felt His life flourishing inside her. She looked around her garden and began to see wonderful colors appear. It thrilled her to see that He was restoring her heart right before her very eyes as she received the truths coming from His words. Instantly she recognized the changes that He was making inside of her were accelerated.

"I am amazed by You," she said, smiling at Him.

He kissed her forehead and said, "You will receive a total of twelve stones on this journey. Each will touch your heart in a special way and be a memorial to you, Ally. And when others ask, 'What do these stones mean to you?' you can tell them of the things the Lord's hand has done to replant and restore your life. All the people I orchestrate for you to touch will know that My hand is mighty, and they too will be changed and worship Me forever."

He looked into her eyes.

He said, "Ally, your life and My life *in* you will cause others to want Me and worship Me forever!"

"Recreate me with Your love, Lord," Ally prayed.

Her prayer touched His heart.

Her willingness to be transformed to look like Him to the world ravished His being.

They both began to sing one of Ally's favorites:

> *Amazing Grace, how sweet the sound*
> *That saved a wretch like me.*
> *I once was lost, but now I'm found,*
> *Was blind, but now I see.*[2]

DEVOTIONAL GUIDE 16

"The thought of being healed and sharing with others that they might also be healed simply sounds too good to be true, Jesus. However, letting You into my garden feels like the healing waters from the River of Life are beginning to flow within. Is that true, Jesus?"

Jesus gleefully answered, "Your heavenly Father made you beautiful and beloved. God invested an incredible amount of effort and concentration in designing you. You are unique, one of a kind. God has thought extensively about you. He smiled on the day He created you."

"What went wrong, Jesus? Why do I have such brokenness within the garden of my soul?"

Jesus continued, "Pain and suffering came as a consequence of the Fall. We will talk more about that later. For now I want you to know if you will let Me heal your pain and trauma, I will not only reign in you, but you will also reign with Me. I will reign in your heart and actually use what the enemy did to make you stronger; and I will cause a river of living water from which others can drink and be healed to flow out of you. Remember the Kingdom of God is within you because you have received Me as your Savior. Please receive a bouquet of roses right now instead of the ashes from trauma as a deposit of more to come. We shall begin replacing the doom within with a praising, joyful heart."

"I receive, Jesus. This is such good news."

(Consider the following Scriptures: Isaiah 61:1-3; Luke 17:21; and 2 Timothy 2:12. Write down what you are coming to understand.)

My Garden Within

_____

_____

_____

Devotional Guide Inventory Chapter 4

1. In whose image were you created? Whose DNA is in your inner being? Who is the only One who can bring about your potential? Had you ever thought about these facts before? Which truth means the most to you?

2. What comes to mind when you hear the word *repentance*? What do your realize about repentance after studying your devotional? Is repentance based on how many tears you shed? What is it about?

3. Have you been tormented by unkind, discouraging, hateful words hurled at you? Have you believed them? How can this belief be changed? How is this different from the ways you have tried to change yourself in the past?

4. How can suffering and trauma be turned for good? Does this seem impossible? Who does the impossible—God or humans? How can this truth not only benefit you but also others?

My Garden Within Inventory

_____

_____

_____

_____

_____

_____

_____

_____

_____

_____

_____

_____

_____

_____

_____

_____

_____

_____

_____

_____

CHAPTER 5

Foundation

For no other foundation can anyone lay than that which is [already] laid, which is Jesus Christ (the Messiah, the Anointed One) (1 Corinthians 3:11).

A few days had passed since Ally had chosen to come into the secret place of her garden. So when she entered, she was a little leery that Jesus would be upset with her. She walked around, looking at the work the Holy Spirit and Jesus had continued in her absence.

She was a little confused and thought, *Why are They still working on my garden? I haven't even taken the time to meet with Them.*

She sat down on a rock and took in a deep breath, admiring the beauty that was being formed in and around her. It still looked to be dead in quite a few areas of her soul, though, and a bit crowded in others.

Those must be the places in my life that need the pruning Jesus mentioned, she thought.

She heard laughter from across her garden, so she got up and followed the sound. She came to a place in her garden where all she could see was a large area of dry land with no growth. Dirt. Just dirt. It was then she saw Jesus on the horizon. She walked for what felt like miles through the dirt to meet with Him. The voice of laughter was still resounding through this dry land.

He then saw her coming and ran to her. He lifted her up and spun her around, still laughing.

Ally tried to join with Him but still felt guilty for not spending any time with Him.

"Why are You so happy?" she asked.

As He set her down, He spoke, "Because today is foundation day, Ally," He replied. "And there is no greater joy to Me than My Father's love, which is the foundation for which everything else grows here. It is the day that He is establishing this firm foundation in you."

"But weren't You upset with me for not coming here for a while?" she asked, her countenance full of shame and regret.

Then He spoke a truth to her heart that resounded across the desert land in her and began to loosen the dirt around her. Even beneath her feet she felt the ground was shifting.

He said, "I want to put more revelation and understanding in your life today. I want to imprint on your heart and to establish firmly in your mind that the reality and the strength of your life is not your commitment to Me, but My commitment to you!" He smiled from ear to ear.

DEVOTIONAL GUIDE 17

"Jesus, I love learning to walk with You as a way of life, but my habits of not regularly reading Your Word very often makes me feel like I am not worthy to receive Your love. The guilt, shame, and regret almost consume me. Please help me."

Jesus smiled with excitement as He answered, "My special love, My love is yours because you are 'in Me' not because of your performance. This truth is missed by so many of Father's children. That is one of the main lies the enemy spews upon humankind.

"Now, My love, let this truth sink deeply within. Any *condemnation*, whether it is feeling disapproved of, unfit for use, shame, regret or guilt, is not from Me. Refuse those thoughts. When I want to correct your path, the Holy Spirit will convict you of destructive ways and show you how to cooperate with Me to move you forward in My love. He does not condemn.

"As you get to know Me through companionship and reading My Word, you see the truth and are set free. Now, I want to bless your human spirit to know the truth deep within your heart. Your human spirit came alive to Me when you received Me as your Savior. Your human spirit is how We communicate with you. Your soul then interprets the truth into this realm of time and space. Your body manifests what you are learning. Through this flow you come to wholeness.

"Now, I bless your human spirit to identify yourself as God's very own beloved child, securely loved in your Abba's family. I bless you with belonging, inclusion, and worth that your Father's love nurtures in you." (Abba is the Hebrew word for father. Hebrew is the language in which the Old Testament Scriptures were originally written.)

"Jesus, knowing how You feel about me is so comforting. I receive."

(Bask in these Scriptures, letting Jesus' love be received and established in you: Jeremiah 31:3; Romans 8:1; and 1 Thessalonians 5:23. Spend extra time letting the above blessing of your human spirit sink deeply within your heart. Write down your thoughts.)

My Garden Within

_____

_____

_____

He then said, "When you gave your heart to Us, to the Father, to Me, and to the Holy Spirit, We made a commitment to change you into Our very image. And Our continuing in your garden, Our creation of this life in you, is unconditional. It's unconditional of you coming because We know you will come back; it is in you now to come, because We know that nothing else satisfies. We are shaping you by Our unconditional love. We love you because We created you. When you gave Us back your heart, you gave Us back the ability to form you into Our image and to create fruit and life in you."

Ally was amazed at the progress and the life she felt instantly in her as He spoke.

"This soil beneath your feet is the foundation from which everything else grows. This soil is the unconditional love of God, and when you understand and receive the love of God, everything else just grows! God loves you. We love you!"

He took her arms, put them in the waltz position, and began to dance with her—just like Cinderella and her prince. Ally laughed. There, in the desert place, they danced, and His love continued to grow in her heart.

DEVOTIONAL GUIDE 18

"Thank You, Jesus, for beginning my freedom journey. Now, I want to read Your Word to get to know You, not because I have to earn Your approval. What a relief!"

"What a delight to see you understand My heart, My love." Jesus gently spoke, "Take in My Word from Jeremiah 15:16, *'Your words were found, and I ate them, and Your words were to me a joy and the rejoicing of my heart, for I am called by Your name, O Lord, God of hosts.'*"

Jesus continued, "My love, I want you to not only know Me, but to also know the joy of learning who I am and how practical I am in your life. I would like you to starting asking yourself this question when you start to struggle in any area, *What is it about Jesus I do not know, that if I knew I wouldn't be struggling as I am with* _____*?* For instance, if you doubt My love, let My word from Romans 8:32 (NKJV) sink into your heart, crushing all doubt, *'He who did not spare His own Son, but delivered Him up for us all, how shall He not with Him also freely give us all things?'* Or should you struggle with My goodness meditate upon My words written down in Psalm 119:68, *'You are good and kind and do good; teach me Your statutes.'* As you eat My words that address your struggle, My words hammer down the walls of unbelief and bring healing.

"My special love, I want to once again bless your human spirit for enlargement and strength. I bless you with being convinced deeply in your spirit that nothing in heaven, earth, or hell can separate you from your Father's love. I bless you with knowing this truth, that nothing in your past, present, or future can take His love from you. Receive and abide deeply in these truths."

"Jesus, I embrace Your unconditional love. How amazing."

(Meditatively read the following Scriptures: Romans 8:31-39; Psalm 119:68; and Jeremiah 15:16; 23:29. Let the blessing of your human spirit become yours. Write down what He is saying to you.)

My Gaden Within

_____

_____

_____

Intimacy

"We love your soul!" He exclaimed. "Intimacy with Me breaks up this hard, uncultivated ground."

He shuffled His feet in the hard ground of her heart. "Move your feet. Do you feel the ground? It is softening as you are here with Me."

Ally shuffled her feet and giggled.

"Do you remember what I said grows in hard, uncultivated ground? Weeds. Where there are no seeds there are weeds. So we need to plant some seeds! Seeds are truth, and truth brings forth life."

He held out His hands toward heaven, and an abundance of seeds started falling from the sky and filled both of His hands to overflowing.

"These seeds need more good soil, because good soil creates strong roots." He threw the seeds in the air. "So let's look at how we can make the soil good."

He sat in the dirt and, pulling Ally down to sit with Him, picked up some dirt and let it drop slowly to the ground. "In a natural garden, if the ground is hard and unfertilized and not watered, growth will stop, and it could eventually die. Cultivating, which is spending time with Me, promotes the growth of the seeds and the existing plants in your garden. Preparing this soil before planting by basking in the unconditional love of our Father is better than trying to get something to grow in bad soil. Remember, His love is the foundation from which everything else grows to its potential for giving out, and it refreshes others for life."

Ally began to get excited. She said, "So what You are saying is that by seeking You, and by being with You here in the secret place of my garden, being intimate with You here, getting to know You here, and believing that You love me unconditionally—that is the foundation that will make the ground of my heart soft and pliable again and ready for growth?"

Jesus grinned and said, "Yes, that is exactly what I am saying. Your part is to crave Me with all your heart, as your soul's first necessity, because you will crave what you feed yourself the most, and your appetite for Me will grow as you spend time with Me."

Ally thought about that statement for a while. She thought, *When I begin to eat a lot of sugar, I crave more sugar, and when I watch too many movies, I begin to crave them. So if I spend time with Jesus, I will begin to crave Him, and I will begin to have an intense desire for Him.*

DEVOTIONAL GUIDE 19

"Learning about working in the dirt is really new to me, Jesus. When I work in the soil of my natural flower garden, I do not enjoy getting dirty, hot, and sweaty. Help me to see how You have so much joy working with the dirt of my life."

Jesus quoted from His Word in Hebrews 12:2 His answer, *"Looking unto Jesus, the author and finisher of our faith, who for the joy that was set before Him endured the cross, despising the shame, and has sat down at the right hand of the throne of God"* (NKJV).

Jesus went on to explain, "Enduring the shame and suffering by way of the cross that you might become whole was not fun. I made it through that hell because of the joy I would receive when you receive My love and learn to walk with Me as a way of life."

I respond, "Yes, that is a similar thing. I put up with being dirty when I work in my garden because I anticipate the beautiful blooms and fragrance my natural garden will give to me. Now, I am beginning to understand."

Jesus said, "Let Me bless your spirit once again with Father's love. Father says you are His gold mine. He has placed within you your own special, wonderful, unique identity. You have divine legitimacy straight from His heart. He is pleased with who He created you to be. He will provide everything you need to live out your birthright confidently and purposefully. May your spirit be revived to receive the Father-heart of God."

"I am basking in what You have shared, Jesus. I choose to believe You. I will meditate upon these truths allowing the Holy Spirit to make them real to me."

(After reading Hebrews 12:1-2, Romans 8:14-17, and Ephesians 1:17-18, write down your insights. Drink in the above blessing of your spirit until it strengthens your inner being.)

My Garden Within

_____

_____

_____

She looked to Jesus and said, "Teach me."

They stood up and walked across the dirt-filled meadow, and Jesus said, "One of the ways you prepare your soil, your heart, is to be aware of what you are saying. You need to let no ugly, unattractive, offensive, or dishonest words come from your mouth."

They stopped and He turned her to face Him. "Do not contaminate your soil with polluting words. If the soil gets contaminated, things will not grow in it. You can pollute the soil in your heart by what you speak. Even self-talk, the things you say to yourself, can damage your soil. For example, when you say, 'I'm stupid' or 'I'm so fat' or 'I always drop things,' these words can harm the soil of your heart. Negative language can clog or obstruct the flow of God in your life, Ally. Negative self-talk also entangles like a weed. It tries to kill the life in you, and it affects who you are."

Ally watched Him as He bent down and freed a little petunia that was being choked by a ragweed. The petunia seemed to thank Him with its freely swaying stem. Ally thought about how many times a day she thought or spoke badly to herself, about herself or others. She thought of these things that did not bring or produce life.

Jesus continued, "The discharge of harmful words can create a polluted atmosphere."

"So our words to ourselves and others can change the very atmosphere we live in for the better or the worse?" Ally questioned.

"Yes. Your words can either bring life or death to yourself or those who hear you," He replied.

"Oh Lord, let the words of my mouth and the meditation of my heart be pleasing to You," she pleaded.

DEVOTIONAL GUIDE 20

"Why has the atmosphere become so polluted, Jesus?"

"When others chose their will over My will; pollution, wounds, unmet needs and suffering entered humankind. We knew this would happen. However, to have sons and daughters for Father and a Bride for Myself, freedom of choice had to be given. I paid the price for all those bad choices.

"Now, My love, you can judge what comes from the enemy and what comes from Father. Father gives only good gifts. I like the way My

Word describes this in James 1:17-18 (MSG): *'So, my very dear friends don't get thrown off course. Every desirable and beneficial gift comes out of heaven. The gifts are rivers of light cascading down from the Father of Light. There is nothing deceitful in God, nothing two-faced, nothing fickle. He brought us to life using the true Word, showing us off as the crown of all his creatures.'*

"Please listen with your spirit to God's Word for you, so you may receive Father's kind intention toward you. *'As the Father has loved Me, so have I loved you. Now remain in My love' 'I have told you this so that My joy may be in you and that your joy may be complete.'"*

"Jesus, I choose Your will and Father's kind intention toward me. Thanks for making this possible."

(Bask in these truths from John 15:9, 11 (NIV) until joy begins to bloom in your soul. Write down your response.)

My Garden Within

_____

_____

_____

Jesus kneeled down, and as He reached His hand toward the dirt, a little white daisy popped through the soil and grew up to meet Him. He picked it and handed it to Ally. "If you plant in the soil of your mind good thoughts and words, the harvest that comes out of it will be amazing to you," He said.

Ally smiled at the tiny daisy, and it seemed to smile back at her.

"Soil," Jesus continued, "is a complex mixture of diverse ingredients containing all the nutrients that sustain life. My job as the Gardener of your soul is to keep the soil in the best possible condition for receiving or giving and to replace the nutrients that plants have taken up. This takes spending time with Me."

He took Ally's face into His hands. "I replace love when you give it. Don't be afraid to love."

Her eyes filled with tears, because she knew she was a little afraid to love again.

He of course knew this already and continued, "I replace lies with truth."

She felt His truth beginning to free her that very moment. Jesus again sat in the dirt of Ally's heart and began to make a pile with His hands. She sat down next to Him.

"To make the best use of the soil in your garden, you should know its properties. You need to know what's in it before you can improve it. You must know its deficiencies. What is it lacking? Is it lacking love, patience, kindness, gentleness, joy, or maybe some self-control? Is it void of peace and faith?" He looked to Ally.

Ally inquired, "Oh Lord, what is in my heart? What in here is good? What is lacking? What is hurting or polluting the soil of my heart? What lies are planted there? What truths? What life? Please show me."

DEVOTIONAL GUIDE 21

"I have felt so alone, so useless, so unworthy and that I have been completely ruined for so long, Jesus. How do I replace the truth for the lies that have tormented me?"

"I am so glad you asked, My special love. My Word says in Jeremiah 15:19, and I quote, *'If you return [give up this mistaken tone of distrust and despair], then I will give you again a settled place of quiet and safety, and you shall be My minister; and if you separate the precious from the vile [cleansing your own heart from unworthy suspicions concerning God's faithfulness], you shall be as My mouthpiece.'*

"For instance, when you hear 'there is no hope for you,' know that is from the enemy who wants to destroy you. Replace that lie by saying, 'Jesus is my hope.' Or, when you hear, 'You are not loved,' say the truth from My Word, 'Yes I am loved because God loved me so much He gave His only Son for me.' Are you beginning to understand how to replace lies with truth, My special love?"

"Yes, Jesus. I am going to start right now feasting upon Your Word for my life. I will 'chew' on these truths until they are part of me."

(Meditate upon Jeremiah 15:19, John 3:16, and 1 Thessalonians 5:21-22. Write down what speaks to you. Review these thoughts until you feel you have received all you need for now.)

My Garden Within

_____

_____

_____

"As you spend time with Me, My love will reveal all this to you. You will know in the days ahead what is needed. My precious Holy Spirit will be speaking to you in every situation and in every word spoken from your mouth. If you listen, We will teach you. In every moment, even in the mundane ones, We are there. Talk to Us. We love it when you glance in Our direction. That is worshipping Us, even when you look Our way for only a moment, knowing We are right there with you."

Ally smiled, and every part of her being smiled with her in that moment. She thought, *He loves me. He loves me!*

She then shouted, "You love me!" and jumped into Jesus' arms.

He held her there for a moment, but even when He set her down, she still felt held. Dirt began to fall from the sky.

"What is this?" Ally asked.

"Sometimes more dirt is needed in your garden. His unconditional love is the new dirt, and it is filled with everything you need for life and godliness. It is more foundation. It is more love," Jesus answered.

Ally raised her hands, and the dirt falling from the sky filled them instantly, just as it was filling her heart. When she pulled her dirt-filled hands to herself, she looked into them and saw a little brown stone that looked to have layers. She pulled it out of the dirt and blew on it to get the residue off. *It's so shiny,* she thought.

"This is your foundation stone, Ally," Jesus said as He smiled, "a memorial to you that the foundation from which everything grows is the unconditional love of God."

Ally pulled from her pocket the little black pouch that contained her first stone and added this second stone to it. She held the pouch close to her chest, took a deep breath, and began that day with a new foundation under her feet.

God loves me!

DEVOTIONAL GUIDE 22

"Jesus, unconditional love seems too good to be true. You mean You will never stop loving me no matter what I do? How can that be?"

"My special love, it is so true. You can do nothing to make Me love you more and nothing to make Me love you less. I never change. I am the same yesterday, today, and forever. I am love. Even though you have sinned, the Father loves you and asks you to sit together with Me at His right hand because you are in Me.

"Look around you at the creative and unique reminders of your Father's love for you. Remember the time you found a lily blooming in your natural garden that you didn't remember planting? It was a special reminder that He was communicating His love to you. Observe the new sunset He paints for you each evening. I bless you My special love to receive the communication of His love to you in the many thousand ways He uses. I bless you with knowing deep in your spirit that your Father's favor is upon you. Not only is His favor upon you, but He likes you."

"Jesus, I am overwhelmed with the thought that You and Father really like me and love me unconditionally. I will ponder this with great delight."

(Soak in His Word to you in Malachi 3:16, Hebrews 13:5-8, and Ephesians 2:5-10. What are your thoughts? Write them down for future consideration and digestion. Spend extra time marveling not only in the truth of Jesus' special love but also the fact that He likes you.)

My Garden Within

_____

_____

_____

Devotional Guide Inventory Chapter 5

1. Is it difficult to believe that anyone, especially God, loves you no matter what you do or have done? Did you know that condemnation, shame, and other associated emotions are not from God? Have you ever realized your human spirit needed to be strengthened and enlarged? Have you considered doing so by blessing your human spirit with the truth?

2. What do you understand is the reason for reading God's Word? As the Holy Spirit guides you while reading, what kind of results should happen? How does it make you feel to know nothing can separate you from God's love? Have you considered this before?

3. What was Jesus' focus while suffering your hell on the cross? What should be your focus while facing past or present pain? Did you realize you have a gold mine of treasurers within to show you your identity and legitimacy? Ask the Holy Spirit to begin opening your eyes to who you are in Him.

4. What is the source of pain and suffering in the world? How can you reverse the curse that came from bringing sin into the world through wrong choices? How can you bring joy into your life?

5. Did you realize there was a place of quiet and safety in which you can dwell? How do you determine what is precious and what is vile? How do you "chew" upon His Word as an assimilation process?

6. Did you realize Jesus will never stop loving you? What are you seeing about His love and why this is true? Ask God to open your eyes to the many ways in which He loves you.

My Garden Within Inventory

_____

_____

_____

_____

_____

_____

_____

_____

_____

_____

_____

_____

_____

_____

_____

_____

_____

_____

_____

_____

_____

_____

CHAPTER 6

Purpose

*For God so loved the world that he gave his one and only Son,
that whoever believes in him shall not perish but have eternal
life* (John 3:16 NIV).

Above them the clouds began to swirl. Ally and Jesus heard these words from heaven, and they realized quickly that it was their Father's voice.

"I so loved the world, and I so loved you, Ally, that I gave My only Son, that if you believe in, trust in, and cling to Him, you will never perish but have everlasting life!"

Ally's heart was touched by His words; she realized that God was saying that her Jesus had taken her place in death so that she would never experience death, and that when she did leave this world, she would take her last breath here and her first breath in eternity. She grasped the reality that He had given His life to her—a life eternal and everlasting.

As Ally and Jesus continued to look toward the sky above them, the voice seemed to take on a form. It was the form of a rainbow, but it differed in that each color that formed on the bow was made from various gems—rubies, sapphires, different colored diamonds, and emeralds. These precious stones from heaven began to descend and then formed again right over Jesus, and Jesus spoke to Ally.

"Yes, I have loved you with an everlasting love; therefore with loving-kindness have I drawn you and continued My faithfulness to you. I knew you from heaven, Ally, before you were ever born, and again I will build you up, and I will adorn you. And yes, you were an afflicted garden. Your soul had been lashed by the storms that have come into your life, and you were not comforted. But I have come into your soul, and I will build you with these gems surrounding me," He said.

He pointed to the rainbow above His head. "I am building in you a spiritual infrastructure that cannot be destroyed or even shaken by the storms. Too often, Ally, have you constructed your own life on the sinking foundations of lies and false assumptions, and the city you were building without Me involved was poised for collapse. But I am going to build within you walls made up of the precious stones of My solid truths, and you will be able to withstand all the storms of life that come your way."

DEVOTIONAL GUIDE 23

"Jesus, my mind is spinning trying to embrace all You have done for me and are offering to me. I have never had anyone love me so much. Help me to grasp all You and Father are saying."

"Your receiving heart is all that is required My love. Remember, I told you your spirit came alive to Me when you received Me as your Savior?"

"Yes, my Lord. What does that really mean?"

"I placed a new heart in you at that time. When you live in My presence, relying upon and trusting Me, your new heart is activated and comes alive. As you receive the truth from My Word via the Holy Spirit, believe it rather than the lies that others or the enemy has told you, and your progress of wholeness and liberty from bondage will begin. Listen to My words from Ezekiel 11:19-20, *"I will give them one heart [a new heart] and I will put a new spirit within them; and I will take the stony [unnaturally hardened] heart out of their flesh, and will give them a heart of flesh [sensitive and responsive to the touch of their God], that they may walk in My statues, and keep My ordinances, and do them. And they shall be My people, and I will be their God."*

"Jesus, I want my heart, which has been hardened by lies and wounds, to be replaced by the new heart You gave me. I agree to diligently walk in Your presence with a cooperative spirit so You can do the work in the garden of my soul."

(Meditate upon 2 Corinthians 5:17, Ezekiel 11:19-20, and Hebrews 8:10, asking the Holy Spirit to open the eyes of your heart. Write down the insights you glean from these Scriptures.)

My Garden  Within

_____

_____

_____

He took Ally's hands and began to dance with her. "You will dance here with Me always, and I will plant vineyards upon the mountains. In every difficult place in your life, We will plant there! The Father and I, We will grow the fruit in you to be given to others to enjoy and to truly live. You will give out this true life that you have been given, and you will live it out, and many will see it. They will see Me and be saved!"

Ally's breath was taken away by the beauty of the rainbow surrounding Jesus; her heart was ravished by Him and His presence. Then she turned to see some mountains in her garden.

Following her gaze, He said, "These mountains in your garden represent difficulties in your life. They portray the deep anguish you feel in your soul and the damage in your garden because of your past. But that very place is where We want to plant vineyards and where We want to plant Our truths in you."

That pleased Ally's heart. *My Jesus is going to continue growth in me as I choose to stay and abide in Him, and He will use me to give life, His very life, to others,* she thought.

Just then, this life began springing up all around her, and the once dirt-covered meadow turned into a vineyard as she stood in the midst of it. As far as she could see were rows and rows of grapevines that were lush and filled with succulent red grapes. She realized that the physical appearance of Jesus was not present anymore, but she knew completely that He was still in her midst—that He was the life springing up around her.

He was building and planting in her for a purpose. He was restoring her soul.

Then Ally again heard the Father in heaven speak these words: "I *am* the artist of this vineyard, this garden within you. You, Ally, are My workmanship. I am fashioning you for this world to bring Me glory. I am fashioning you to set you as My display, and I will say, 'Look at My daughter. The presence of My Son is being formed in her. Isn't He beautiful in her'?"

Ally was amazed that God was boasting about her and proud of her— and that He saw His Son in her. She began to bite her lip.

DEVOTIONAL GUIDE 24

"Mountains made of unmet needs, wounds, or unresolved issues seem to be crushing me, Jesus. How do I begin to remove these mountains?"

Since nothing is too hard for Jesus, He immediately said, "My special love, I am delighted to guide you as We either immediately remove the mountain, go over it, or through it. Either way it shall be removed.

"Let's start with the most important step. Realize staying in relationship with Me is the healing way of processing any problem or trauma. When a lie seeks to torment you or a painful memory comes to mind, intentionally turn to Me. Focus upon remembering the most comforting time, thought, or experience you have ever had. Stay there with Me until your soul is quiet and knows I am your safe place. Then, give that lie, fear, or memory to Me asking Me what I want you to know about this mountain?

"Realize My special love, I may immediately give you a thought, picture, word of comfort, or insight, or it may be later through someone else, My Word, a dream or one of the many other ways in which I communicate. Regardless, know I am listening. I will enable you to process this mountain. Continue to walk in that settled place of quiet and safety. As we do this, we will get to know each other more intimately. You will look more and more like Me."

"Yes, Jesus, I will begin giving to You my problems and pain, and allow You to begin settling them within me, as we navigate through them together. What an amazing adventure."

(Start this process by remembering the safest, most comforting time in your life as your place to go when you need it. Study Psalms 37:7-8; 46:10 and Matthew 17:20; 21:21-22. Record your thoughts.)

My Gaden Within

---

Then God said, "I sent My Son with a purpose for you, Ally—to die on your behalf and actually live your life for you. Your purpose in this life is to *let Him* live His life through you and let Him live *in* you. The way I reach My world now is through you, My believers. Will you be My hand extended, Ally? Will you allow My love to be poured forth through you? Will you walk with Me and for Me? For this is My purpose for you: to form My beautiful Son within you and to form My life in you."

Ally felt so much warmth in her heart and so much adoration for her Jesus.

"That is why He came to the earth. He came to die for you and in place of you so that you could truly live and live forever," God said.

Ally turned to one of the vines forming in her, and she noticed a huge cluster of grapes. She picked one of the grapes from the cluster, and it changed in the palm of her hand into a luscious red ruby. She recognized that this was the third memorial stone, and she instantly knew the meaning of this one. This stone represented Jesus' death on her behalf and the blood He shed was for her so that she could live a life forever with Him and for Him.

She clutched the little stone tightly. Then she pulled the black pouch from her pocket and added the ruby to the existing precious promises of God. She kissed toward heaven, put the pouch back in her pocket, and she continued with her day with His step in her gait.

DEVOTIONAL GUIDE 25

"Jesus, I remember You said that I cannot live the Christian life in my own strength. The Christian life is lived as I trust You and walk in Your presence. You flow through me. Can You help me understand this?"

"All your questions are good ones, My special love. When Adam opened the door of sin by choosing his will not Mine, pain and suffering started flowing and multiplying. The ravages of sin manifested through the act of Cain murdering his brother Abel. Since that time Abel's blood has cried out to Me from the ground upon which it fell. At the cross when My blood dropped to the ground, the redemption process was activated. Each time the blood is trusted and applied, the curse is reversed. All suffering can now be turned to gain for you and My Kingdom. My blood flows through you as you walk with Me. My life is in My blood. My blood makes you fully alive as we journey together. My life within the garden of your soul heals and replaces the darkness with My life and light. My handiwork begins to be obvious in and through you. Isn't that good news?"

"Jesus, You always share such good news with me. I have much to ponder and embrace."

(Ponder the following Scriptures and record your thoughts: Genesis 4:1-11; Leviticus 17:11; Romans 3:24-26; 5:12; Hebrews 9:13-14; 10:14.)

My Garden Within

_____

_____

_____

She realized after this time spent with Him in the secret place of her garden that she had almost forgotten about a previous engagement. She was supposed to meet four of her friends at a nearby coffee shop. These were four friends who had known her for quite some time. They knew her, so to speak, in her weaknesses.

When she arrived at the coffee shop, she saw the four sitting at a quaint little table in the corner. She sat down and began conversing with them. Something in her countenance captivated her small audience. They began noticing and commenting on the attractiveness of her person.

"What is going on with you?" one of them questioned.

"Well," Ally said, "I have met the One whom my soul loves. I have been spending time with Jesus in the secret place."

Of course her friends had heard of Jesus; they knew *of* Him, but they did not know Him.

Ally covered her heart with her hands. "He has been showing me that the secret place is within me, and it is in the garden of my soul. There I have been meeting with Him, and He has been healing me and my emotions and restoring me," Ally said.

She patted her heart twice. "You see, He showed me that I am His—that I am His garden and that He is mine, that He really is alive, and that He is alive in me." She smiled. "It has been a really amazing journey with Him," she said, looking at them, right into their eyes. "He has captivated my heart in every way."

Her friends just sat there, amazed at her words, which came from her heart. They were astonished at the transformation that they were seeing in her.

She continued to tell them all of what the Lord had done and said and was continuing to do. They were so interested in the remarkable person whom their friend had championed with such unstinting praise, and they too wanted to know Him.

One friend then said, "Can we too know Him like this? Where is He? For we would seek Him with you."

Another one said, "This is beautiful, and you are beautiful, Ally. I see this new life changing you before our eyes. I think I see Him in your eyes right now."

Ally replied, "The eyes are the gateway to the soul. That is where He is, my Jesus. That is why you can see Him in my eyes."

By this time all of her friends' eyes had welled up with tears.

"Where is He, you ask?" She looked at each of them. "He is here, with us right now. He is in the midst of us. He can live in you also; all you need to do is ask."

Ally smiled and continued to hold her hands to her heart. "Just ask Him in. He will come. His desire is to come. His desire is to restore, heal, and love us back into wholeness so that we can in turn pour out that same love to others."

As she gazed at her friends, they all now had tears streaming down their faces. She heard Jesus speak to her heart.

"These women are the first fruits from your dream. You are awakening their hearts to Me, and they too are for the first time realizing their purpose and their worth in Me and to Me," He said.

Ally then held out her hands to her friends. "Can we pray?" she asked.

DEVOTIONAL GUIDE 26

"Jesus, I am beginning to believe and hope there is a chance for me to be whole. I want to tell others, but I still feel so broken at times. How can I be used for others when I feel tainted and ruined myself?"

"Thank you, My special love, for asking this significant question," Jesus said while smiling. "This is a universal question My enemy uses to keep My good news from being released. You can share with others because you are in Me and I am the perfect One…not you. They are not inviting you into their lives but Me. I died so everyone can have My resurrection life, which is a far better life than anyone can ever live on their own.

"Through My blood the world was squared with Father giving them a chance for a fresh start when they receive the forgiveness of sins that I offer. Now, I have given you the task of telling everyone what We have done for them. You are My representative of reconciliation. As you tell everyone to drop their differences and enter into God's work of making things right between them, We all win. You are blessed by sharing about Me and those who receive also become His trophies of grace. Isn't that good news?"

"Yes, Jesus, that is good news. I am excited about being Your representative of reconciliation. I look forward to the ways You will show me to share and what to say."

"One more thought on this subject, My special love. When you share what I am doing in your life, whether it is in a conversation or speaking to a group, don't be surprised if the enemy comes to taunt you, seeking to stop your sharing. Thoughts may come that you didn't do it right, or that you messed up, or you are not good enough to share. The enemy is simply trying to keep you from telling My good news. As you turn to Me during this time of attack, I will use it to establish you in Me, knowing it is about Me, not about you doing it perfectly. Keep sharing. Keep telling the enemy that your God is big enough to handle your imperfections. We win! That's what makes the enemy so mad."

(Prayerfully read 2 Corinthians 5:12-21. After you have meditated upon these verses, write down what you are beginning to understand.)

My Garden Within

---

They all kind of looked around and then at each other, shrugged their shoulders, and joined their hands with one another.

Ally began to pray, saying, "Oh my Jesus, who dwells in the gardens, my companions have been listening to Your voice through me. Now cause them to hear it for themselves. Come into the gardens of their souls and live. Live in them from this day forward. Allow them to hear You call to them to come away with You and to spend time in the secret place, because that is so imperative in these days. Let them know You as I have come to know You—as their healer and their deliverer, as their high tower where they can seek shelter with You and be safe. Fill them with Yourself now. In Your name, amen."

They all sat quietly in His sweet presence for a while. The coffee shop seemed to have come to a standstill. It was as if they had been lifted into a whole new realm, a totally different place.

Then Ally joyfully found herself in the garden of her soul again. She turned to see Him, Jesus, and she prayed aloud with her friends once again.

"To the One altogether lovely, the Chief among ten thousand, no one else can compare to You. My friends are eager to begin a life of sweet companionship with You! Make haste, my Beloved, and come quickly to them, like a gazelle, like a young deer. Take them to Your secret place within them, the garden of their souls, and live in them. Make Yourself known in them, I pray."

Ally and her friends just sat for a time in the presence of this newfound life. What was usually just a time of talking in a coffee shop had turned into a life-changing moment for five women. For the One altogether lovely had come to live in each of their hearts. And Ally, well—she was forever changed!

Devotional Guide Inventory Chapter 6

1. Why do you need a new heart? How is this heart activated, strengthened, and its capacity expanded? What have you understood about this process?

2. How do you process difficult or painful situations to take the trauma out of the experience? How does staying in Jesus' presence help? Who is the only One who has life and can give it abundantly? Does solving the problem in your own strength work well?

3. How did sin, suffering, and pain enter humans and the earth? How has the curse of sin upon us and the earth been reversed? Do you realize that when you choose your will as opposed to God's will that you add chaos, suffering, and pain to yourself and others?

4. How did God reconcile the world to Himself? What was the cost of reconciling us to our God? Did you know He chose you to be His representative to tell this good news to others? How can He use you when you are not yet mature?

My Garden Within Inventory

_____

_____

_____

_____

_____

_____

_____

_____

_____

_____

_____

_____

_____

_____

_____

_____

_____

_____

_____

_____

_____

_____

CHAPTER 7

Life

I have come that they may have life, and have it to the full
(John 10:10 NIV).

Ally was beginning to experience Jesus more and more in her daily tasks. He was becoming clearer and more evident in her life. His voice was becoming familiar in her ears. For the first time in her life He was real and alive, and she knew Him. She closed her eyes, and immediately she was in a walled garden. It was her garden; she knew this because it had grown so familiar to her. Yet here now was this beautiful wall. It was constructed from stones that were not cut with human hands. It was an amazing sight. Moss of the brightest green covered its face. The mortar that held the stones together had cracks in it, and little white-faced baby daisies were growing from within the cracks. Bees buzzed around, collecting the nectar from these tiny flowers.

Amazingly, Ally wasn't afraid of the bees as she normally would be. When she finished taking in the sight of this great wall around her heart, she realized she was in a part of her garden that was dead. Old, dry chrysanthemums that once had bloomed with beauty lay brown and ugly at her feet. Rose bushes that had once exuded their sweet fragrance now lay barren and unattractive before her eyes. She could clearly see that winter had taken its toll in this part of her garden and in this part of her life. She bent down and broke off a piece of dry, brittle stem from a princess bush.

His voice behind her startled her, and she spun around to see Him. His smile steadied her heart, and she shrugged her shoulders while looking around at the deadness in her soul.

"You know," He said, "when the winter passes and it's time for a new garden, the first thing you have to do is pull up the dead plants."

He tossed Ally some pink and lime green polka-dot gardening gloves. "You know, the old stuff. We need to take out the old, useless patterns of life so that the new life may come."

He slipped on His gloves, and of course they were manlier in appearance than Ally's little polka-dot ones. Yet He knew she would think the gloves He chose for her were pretty.

Adorable, she thought.

"Ally, picture us trying to plant new life and new flowers without first pulling up the dead things from the past. It wouldn't be very beautiful or attractive to others who pass by, would it?"

She surveyed the ground of her heart, trying to imagine beautiful flowers in the midst of the dead plants. "No, it wouldn't," she responded.

DEVOTIONAL GUIDE 27

"Jesus, I am beginning to see that You and You alone are life. I want You to be my life. However, it is so discouraging to see the deadness in the garden of my soul. I wish You would just instantly make me like You. Would You do that for me?"

Jesus heard the cry of His precious one's heart. He understood completely. He empathically responded, "If I instantly made you like Me, you would not know who you are. It would be like someone who has amnesia. As we walk together moment by moment, you fall in love with Me. You discover who I am in you and you go from strength to strength. It is an exciting, intimate love walk. You might compare it to an exciting treasure hunt.

"My precious one, know I am the Way, the Truth, and the Life. Life is a person—Me! I am in you. We are building a relationship that takes time.

As we face removing dead plants or wrong beliefs that have tormented you, you will see My heart and learn to trust Me more and more. It's an intimate love walk where My joy becomes your joy, and your joy becomes fully mature. I want you to treasure the process as I treasure being with you.

"Listen to My words written down in Luke 21:19, *'By your steadfastness and patient endurance you shall win the true life of your souls.'* Isn't that good news, My precious one? I will release patient endurance as we walk together, talk together, and enjoy being with each other."

"Jesus, all this makes sense. I must concentrate on enjoying the process and learning about You. I lay down my impatience."

(Carefully read John 14:6; 15:11 and Luke 21:19. Trust the Holy Spirit to open your eyes to His truth. Record what you understand.)

My Garden Within

_____

_____

_____

"I want to do a new thing, Ally. I don't want you to consider the things of the past or even remember them." He pulled out a dead hydrangea shrub from the ground of her heart. "I am going to plant in this wilderness and bring water, new life, and new growth. Can you perceive it, Ally? Can you see it?"

He was grinning from ear to ear, because He *could* see it. "All who are in your life will see it. They will know and understand that the hand of the Lord has done this and that I have created this beauty."

Ally was amazed that Jesus could see the finished work in her and that He knew that work would have a positive effect in others' lives.

"You are going to help Me sow, Ally, after we finish pulling these useless, dead things out of your life." He nudged her in a playful manner, motioning for her to start helping.

She pulled on her new, pretty polka-dot gardening gloves and began to help Jesus pull up brown masses of the past in her heart. They worked for what seemed like hours, pulling up good-for-nothing rubbish in Ally's life—useless patterns of words spoken to her, by herself or by others, words and thoughts that had killed the beauty within her. Together they pulled up lies that the enemy had planted.

When they were finished in that particular part of her heart, they stood again in the midst of simple, plain dirt.

"Nothing grows without seed," Jesus said. "If we do not plant something here, we will reap nothing." He pulled a bag of seeds from His shirt pocket. "If you want a new harvest and a new life, you need a new plan and new seeds."

He opened the packet. "If you want new life, you have to throw away your old seed—the way you used to act and the way you used to speak. You need to sow what you haven't sown before."

He scratched His head before speaking again, first looking over her soul. "Look forward to the new field and garden, Ally. Don't look back on the old, but press forward."

She looked around at her heart. "How do I start, Lord?"

"First," He answered, "don't carry or even bring with you the old seeds. Get rid of them—get rid of all the negative seeds! For whatever you sow, only that is what you will reap. If we plant corn seeds, Ally, it will not come up as wheat. If we plant corn, we will reap corn. Does that make sense?"

DEVOTIONAL GUIDE 28

"Jesus, I appreciate getting to know You by learning to walk and talk with You. Help me to understand why You are so hopeful concerning my outcome when I get so easily discouraged."

Jesus is so delighted with the questions that arise from a hungry heart. He smiled with excitement saying, "I understand, My love. You see, I have eternal eyes. I am sitting at the right hand of My Father and We not only see you as a finished Bride of Mine, but We also see how all the things that torment you can be turned for good as you are fitting into Our plan for your life. Remember, nothing is too hard for Us.

"It is hard for you to realize all the beautiful handiwork We are doing in your life. Our part is the transformational handiwork as you simply listen to My voice and obey or participate with what I show you to do. You are developing eternal eyes as you do this. You are seated with Me in heavenly places because you are in Me and that is where I am. As you trust Me by faith, which believes who I am and that I will do what I say, you honor Me and your eyes grow more and more able to see as I see."

"Thanks for sharing this, Jesus. I will soak in Your written Word and ask the Holy Spirit to make it real to me."

(See Romans 8:28, Ephesians 2:6, 10, and 2 Corinthians 5:7. Write down what is meaningful to you.)

My Garden Within

_____

_____

_____

Ally nodded; her brow furrowed as she tried to concentrate and take in what He was saying and sowing into her.

"If you want to reap love and affection, you have to sow love and affection. If you want to reap kindness, you'll have to sow some kindness."

He looked over at the wall in her heart and noticed that the sparrow that had first led her to the entrance of her garden had gotten its little claw caught in a crack. He gently helped set it free.

"And," He said, pouring all of the seeds from the packet into His hand, "you need to sow abundantly. If you want to reap abundantly, you need to sow abundantly." He picked one of the seeds from His palm with His other hand and held it up. "If you only sow this one little seed, what will your garden look like, Ally? Will it be inviting to you or to those who pass by you?"

Ally imagined this huge piece of land before her with just one flower blooming in the middle, and she met Jesus' eyes and smiled.

"I would like to plant more, please," she said, and she giggled.

Jesus then took another route, saying, "The opposite is also true. If you sow to the flesh, you will reap from the flesh."

"What do you mean?" Ally questioned.

"Well, you're either in the presence of the Lord, Me," He said, putting His hand to His chest and smiling, "or you're in the presence of the flesh. You don't have to work at being in the flesh, acting or reacting in an ugly, unattractive way. You don't work to plant weeds, do you?"

Ally understood immediately, thinking, *Sometimes leading a disciplined life is hard. I want to react the way I've always reacted. I just need to tell myself and my flesh, "No, you are not going in that direction today!"*

Jesus heard all her thoughts. "Yes, Ally, discipline seems painful, but afterward, it yields a peaceable fruit of righteousness. Yes, fruit! It conforms you to My plan, My thoughts, and My purposes for your life. When you sow to the Spirit and when you sow to Me, you will be changed into a flourishing garden. You will be full of fruit to be shared with others!"

That made Ally's heart jump. She was so excited to be in this journey with Jesus, this journey to wholeness.

DEVOTIONAL GUIDE 29

"Jesus I want to surrender every part of my human spirit, soul, and body to You. I don't want my flesh to rule. Please elaborate on how this all works in ways that I can more fully cooperate in it with You."

"What a delight it is to Me to do so, My love," Jesus answered. "You see, your soul has survived all these years by doing the best it could.

Surviving is good, but I want you to thrive. To thrive means you have to learn to live in My presence as a way of life. You have to learn to reverse the familiar ways of surviving by thriving through My resurrection life. Old habit patterns are so natural, you often are not aware that you have fallen back into trusting your unredeemed heart. The Holy Spirit will direct you. He may use someone who loves you to remind you that you are not acting like your real, true self. In other words, you are not living from your new heart in Me. At that moment, whether it is the Holy Spirit using someone else, your misery escalating, or conviction showing you that you are out of alignment with Me, you turn and walk back with Me, trusting Me to cleanse and control you through My blood and life. Repentance is turning from the way you were walking and walking now with Me, receiving My grace, which is freely provided.

"My love be patient with yourself. Old habit patterns take at least six weeks to begin reversing. Be very sensitive to the Holy Spirit, applying the discipline necessary to help redirect your thoughts and to choose My way. Reading My Word regularly as well as conversing with Me is important. You will like the results, My love. Trust Me!"

"I choose to thrive rather than simply surviving. Thank You, Jesus, for making this possible."

(Prayerfully read Galatians 6:7-9; 5:24 and Hebrews 12:11. Record what comes to your mind.)

My Garden Within

_____

_____

_____

Preparing the Soil

"Let's go back to cultivating for a moment." He sat on a log that was in her garden, and she sat down next to Him. "Breaking up hard ground after the winter is hard work."

He grabbed a spade that was leaning against the garden wall and jabbed the dirt by His feet with a resounding thud. "Changing the way you act or react in certain situations is hard on the flesh, and you just don't want to work at it. It's hard to control your thoughts and emotions. It's hard work to control your tongue."

He struck the ground with the spade again. "Just like this hard ground—if you don't plow first and soften the hardened ground by choosing to remain in Me, by spending intimate time with Me like we are doing right now, the ground of your heart will remain hard."

Ally reached down and touched the ground of her heart, and her finger didn't even make a dent in the hard dirt.

Jesus said, "Then the roots of your seeds cannot go deep; therefore, the harvest won't be strong." He reached out and turned her face toward Him. "There will be no fruit."

Ally took a deep breath.

"Conforming is hard," He continued, "and you have to be consistent. You need to keep acting right, doing right, and speaking right. You need to talk to yourself and tell your mind and thoughts, 'No, you are not going there today,' and change direction again."

Ally sat, taking it all in.

"Again, Al," He said, "you need to get the foundation right so that you can grow, and that foundation is receiving God's unconditional love for you. Remember, God's love is the foundation from which everything else grows. That's His grace. You can do this as you spend time with Him, Me, the Gardener of your soul."

She smiled at Him because He had shortened her name as she always did with her close friends. He knew that would bless her as He smiled at her. *I love that I am becoming so close to Him that He can give me a nickname,* Ally thought.

Jesus stood up and began to break up the hard ground with the spade. Then He hit a rock. "Sometimes you're going along, breaking up hardened ground, and things are going pretty smoothly. Then you hit a rock, which is a situation or circumstance that the devil, the enemy of your soul, garden, and life, tries to rock your world with." He continued to pry the rock in her heart with His spade. "He's trying to move you away from where you are going and trying to make you go in a different direction—that of doubt, unbelief, or fear. Or maybe he is trying to get you to take up a familiar habit such as anger, unkindness, or a bad behavior. And you just can't plow over these types of rocks, Ally. They have to be removed, or they could break your tools! Or, better said, they could break your life."

Ally reached down and touched the rock in her garden. "It's so big; it looks immovable," she said, and she looked up at Him.

"It may seem immovable, and it will be very hard work to remove it. It is like a stronghold of doubt or a mindset that is trying to stay in your life and in your garden, but it has to be moved!"

Ally thought about some of the things that had taken up residence in her thoughts and in her life: too much television, overeating, addictions, anger, her lack of forgiveness, familiar bad attitudes, old mindsets or labels, and things people had said to her, such as, "You'll never amount to anything" or "What are you, stupid?" *How do I remove these rocks?* she wondered.

"Believe the truth instead of the lie," Jesus said.

Again, He knew her so well.

"Believe what I say about you. Speak that! Consistently speak the truth. Out loud. Say it out loud. There is power in that!"

Ally knew that He was there to help her remove every rock in her soul and her heart that didn't belong. His truth would set her free, and together they removed the one she thought was immovable.

⚜ DEVOTIONAL GUIDE 30 ⚜

"Jesus, I have observed some people who do not know You, who seem to have better control over their thoughts and emotions than I do. How do they do it?"

Jesus said, "My love, let's talk about your question. I gave everyone a will, and they can choose to do good things that make them get along with others and fit into society more smoothly. Some have chosen this way. They fit in more successfully in the world, but the place in their heart that only I can fill is still empty and their good works will have no eternal value.

"Listen to Paul's words in Philippians 3:7-11. He was one of those who according to the world looked like he had it all. He says as translated in the Message, *'The very credentials these people are waving around as something special, I'm tearing up and throwing out with the trash—along with everything else I used to take credit for. And why? Because of Christ. Yes, all the things I once thought were so important are gone from my life. Compared to the high privilege of knowing Christ Jesus as my Master, firsthand, everything I once thought I had going for me is insignificant—dog dung. I've dumped it all in the trash so that I could embrace Christ and be embraced by him. I didn't want some petty, inferior brand of righteousness that comes from keeping a list of rules when I could get the robust kind that comes from trusting Christ—God's righteousness. I gave up all that inferior stuff so I could know Christ personally, experience his resurrection power, be a partner in his suffering, and go all the way with him to death itself. If there was any way to get in on the resurrection from the dead, I wanted to do it.'"*

"How about you, My love?" Jesus asked.

"I agree with Paul, Jesus. I want to surrender every part of me—my spirit, soul, and body."

(Let the Holy Spirit bring about the same convictions within as described by Paul as you read Philippians 3:1-11 from several translations.

My Garden Within

_____

_____

_____

His Living Water Brings Life

They then planted the seeds that Jesus had brought to her garden. They dug little trenches together. Then they carefully placed the seeds one by one and covered them with a light layer of soil.

Jesus said, "After planting the seeds, you water. Every day you water, Ally, even if you don't see anything coming up. If you see no results and no change, you water. You may not see anything coming up for days or weeks, but you keep watering, and you keep speaking life."

As He spoke, He grabbed a hose that was siphoning living water from the River of Life that was within Ally and began sprinkling the newly planted seeds.

"After you plant your seeds, you cannot come and dig them up every few days to see if a crop is coming. Just trust Me, Ally. Trust that I am working, even if you don't see anything coming up yet."

Ally thought of a quote she had recently read: "The answer to prayer may be approaching, though we discern not its coming. The seed that lies underground in winter is taking root in order to a spring and harvest, though it appears not above the ground but seems dead and lost."[1]

Life is coming! She thought. *It is—I am sure of it!*

Jesus then proclaimed over her: "I am giving you a new heart. I am putting My very Spirit within you, and I will take the stony, unnaturally hardened heart out of your flesh and will give to you a heart of flesh. This heart will be sensitive and responsive to My touch."

Ally clutched her chest, and closed her eyes. "Plant in me, Jesus," she pleaded. "Plant the soil in my heart and mind full of good seeds so that the crop and the fruit that comes forth will be nourishing to myself and to others, and life-giving."

Jesus set down the hose and embraced her, and they stood in the silence of the moment. She knew her garden had new seeds and life that very second.

DEVOTIONAL GUIDE 31

"Jesus I plan to water the seeds You are planting. I want the roots to go deep so no problem can uproot the flowers You're releasing within me.

What is a major rock preventing Your living water from bringing forth the fruit we both desire?"

"I am so glad you want to know, My love," Jesus said. "One of the major rocks that We hit is one's lack of forgiveness. Mostly this is because My loved ones do not really understand forgiveness. Forgiveness does not mean what the person did wasn't wrong. Often it was very wrong. What you are doing when you forgive is saying you will release the debt to be paid, and for Me to handle it rather than you requiring payment or retaliation. Since I have clear perspective, I will do what is right for everyone. Just as I have given you forgiveness for what you did wrong, I will extend forgiveness to others if they will receive it. To not forgive is like drinking poison and expecting the other person to die.

"When you forgive, you release yourself from the powerlessness that unforgiveness produces. You are choosing to be controlled by Me and not another's offenses. You are assuming responsibility for your life, for the rest of your life. When you forgive, you can then accept responsibility for your life without blaming others. Evil was done to you. You forgive and we walk together overcoming your present behavior. Becoming responsible is a major step in becoming healed and whole. Forgiveness doesn't mean you have to be reconciled to the one who sinned against you. We will talk more about that later.

"If you are having a very difficult time with My Word that says, *'Beloved, never avenge yourselves, but leave the way open for [God's] wrath; for it is written, Vengeance is Mine, I will repay (requite),' let Me make this suggestion.* When the one you need to forgive comes to mind or the person extends his or her hand to you for forgiveness, say to yourself, 'Jesus forgives through me!' I will do so. My love, whether you feel it or not, you respond as if you do feel forgiveness. That is faith. As you continue in this manner, I will heal the wounded place in your heart. Sometimes healing comes immediately and sometimes it comes later. Trust Me, I know what I am doing."

"With Your strength and empowerment, I choose to walk in forgiveness, Jesus."

(Read what He has to say about this in Romans 12:17-21 and Colossians 3:13. Write down what these words mean to you.)

My Garden Within

_____

_____

_____

The Wall

"You are My walled garden," Jesus said, breaking the silence.

Ally again looked to the daisy-covered stone wall.

"Yours is a garden enclosed," He began, resting His hand on the stone wall, "and this wall is to guard and protect you. Keep and guard your heart and your garden, Ally, for from it come the issues of life."

What are my issues? Ally thought. *If I don't like the way I'm acting, I need to guard what I'm planting or allowing others to plant in me. How do I plant?*

Jesus so loved her thought process. "You plant by speaking right things. Every word spoken is seed. Who is planting in your life, Ally? You need to be cautious of bad seed and of what others may be planting within you. Is what they speak to you truth? Do their words build you up and motivate you? Or do they tear you down and discourage and destroy you? If they speak or plant lies in you, take those words immediately to Me, and I will replace them with My truth. Dig them out before they take root and grow in your heart. You need to take every thought captive, Ally, and guard your heart. Weigh every word spoken to you, or even by you, because the root source of your words is your thoughts. Don't let bad seeds take root. Don't even give them a chance. If you say something negative, say the opposite right away. Stop immediately, and ask the Holy Spirit, 'Is this good seed or bad seed? Will it bring life or death?'"

He then placed His hand on Ally's cheek. "If it's death and hurt, pray this: 'May every plant that my heavenly Father has not planted be torn up by the roots!' I ask you this, Ally: Who are you going to allow to plant in your garden? God? The devil? The world?"

Jesus looked up into the heavens as if He were getting more wisdom poured into Him. He began watering again and said, "See yourself as a walled garden, and protect it. Guard your garden. Supervise all entries and exits, everything that comes in and goes out of your heart or your mouth. For out of the abundance of the heart, your mouth will speak."

Ally put her hand over her mouth, thinking, *He speaks, and truth floods my soul.* She thought about the many times she had let the world dictate her life. The world would issue orders, and she'd just comply. She removed her hand from her mouth.

"I am not going to let the devil or the world and its ways dictate my life anymore!" she said with authority in her voice.

Jesus stopped watering and looked at her. He knew that she was understanding, and that this truth would set her free.

Ally said, "I am seeing that what I take into my heart, I will harvest." She began to tear up. "I have let negativity, worry, insecurity, and fear into my heart and have seen them come up, and even out of me. I want You to dictate my life, Lord. I am ready to sow good things with You and to think on what is pure, holy, and right. I am going to change the seeds I have been planting, and I refuse to be the victim of bad seeds any longer. I am going to guard my eyes and what I look at. I am going to guard my ears, what I hear, and to whom I listen. And last, but definitely not least, I am determined to guard my mouth and what I say. I will speak life to myself and others."

Jesus stepped toward her, dropped the hose, and gently touched her face. He then spoke to her soul, saying, "Your field will change because your seeds have changed. Your garden will change because your seeds have changed. Your life will change because your seeds have changed."

With those words spoken, He took her hand and dropped a seed the shape of a large thorn into her palm. "Life," He said.

Ally looked at the thorn-shaped seed and remembered all He'd done for her when He took the crown of thorns upon His head and died in her place. He had begun to walk away from her in her garden, and again she heard Him from a distance.

"I gave you life," He said.

She looked into her hand at the seed, and it had turned into a beautiful green stone. "Life," she said as she dropped it into her black little pouch with the others.

DEVOTIONAL GUIDE 32

"Jesus, my wall is becoming so beautiful. Can we talk some more about the cracks I placed in my wall and the ones others created that cause problems? I don't want to contribute to tearing down my wall again."

Jesus quickly answered, "My delight is to open your eyes to such truths so you will be free. People who were supposed to protect and nurture you have cooperated with the enemy and abused you with words that were not true, or violated you in other ways. I have hurt with you as you have hurt with this defilement. I paid for each and every wrong done to you when I died in your place on the cross. Now, you and I will partner together to rebuild your wall and renew your mind. As We are walking together you are discovering that I am your fortress, your refuge, your shield, and your high tower. Each time you place your trust in Me, the wall of protection is being secured and solidified.

"The more you walk with Me, the more you recognize the voice and ways of the enemy. As you recognize his lies and evil ways, quickly lead those thoughts to Me. As you release them to Me, I will take them captive. They are secure with Me. Remember; I was given all power in heaven and earth when I ascended to the Father. Also be mindful that wrong ways of responding made deep tracks in your soul and brain that have to be reversed or filled in. Each time you replace the lie with the truth, you fill in the carnal tracks with truth. As we journey this way together, we discover treasures in you and you discover treasures in Me. It's an exhilarating journey or treasure hunt."

"Thank You, Jesus. I am excited about moving forward with You."

(Ponder the following Scriptures: Romans 12:1-2; 2 Corinthians 10:3-6; Psalm 18:1-3, 30; and Matthew 28:18. Write down how these words affect you.)

My Garden Within

_____

_____

_____

Devotional Guide Inventory Chapter 7

1. Have you ever resented or wondered why the process of transformation has to be gradual? What do you now understand is the reason? How does this process come about?

2. Why is Jesus not troubled by your imperfections? What does having eternal eyes mean? How do you gain eternal eyes?

3. What mode do you shift into when you do not know how to walk with Jesus? Survival is better than not surviving, but what does Jesus want for you? When you revert back to old, carnal, familiar habits, what does God use to get your attention and bring you back to thriving? Which ways do you prefer that He use? Why? What is usually the minimum required time to begin replacing old habits with His ways?

4. Does everyone have a will, or the power to choose, as built-in equipment? Can you do good things in your own strength and forfeit eternal value? Why? Do you identify with Paul in his journey of making worldly thinking influence what you do? How? What do you want to see change?

5. What is forgiveness? Who is hurt if you do not forgive? How can you forgive when it is really difficult? Who will take care of the person you forgive? Is God trustworthy to bring about justice for the person you release to Him through forgiveness?

6. How are old habits of your carnal flesh made during your survival mode reversed? How are the tracks or ruts in your brain and soul filled? How can you be patient with yourself during this time?

My Garden Within Inventory

_____

_____

_____

_____

_____

_____

_____

_____

_____

_____

_____

_____

_____

_____

_____

_____

_____

_____

_____

_____

_____

_____

_____

_____

CHAPTER 8

The Vineyard

God has a purpose in view. Often we shrink from the purging and pruning, forgetting the Gardener knows, that the deeper the cutting and paring, the richer the luster that grows.
–L.B. Cowman, *Streams in the Desert*[1]

That evening, Ally was in her home. She had just finished wiping the counters after her meal, and she set her favorite crystal vase filled with pink Gerbera daisies back in the middle of her counter. She looked around her small kitchen and smiled as she prayed, "I'm so thankful, Lord. I can even see You here, in my kitchen, in the natural, mundane things I do every day."

She felt His great peace surrounding her every thought and every move. She ventured into the family room and plopped herself down into her big leather chair that almost seemed to swallow her up. She covered herself with an afghan throw that her mother had made, and she flipped the switch next to her, lighting up the great fireplace. Ally grabbed her Bible, closed her eyes, and prayed.

"Teacher," she began, "teach me." Immediately she flipped through her Bible, and it fell open to John 15. As she read about Jesus being the true vine and how He spoke of His Father as the vinedresser, Ally found herself in the garden of her heart once again.

This particular part of her garden seemed to be very full, even crowded. There seemed to be no more room for growth. Bushes were overgrown and had no definite shape. She could see a tiny part of a path; it was overgrown with wild vines that had left their original form and now grew wherever they desired. *No order*, she thought. She was beginning to feel suffocated.

She looked up. "What is this about, Lord?" she asked.

As she looked back down, Jesus stood in front of her with a huge pair of pruning shears. They had wooden handles that looked to be a bit antique and weathered, and then, of course, there were the sharp blades of the shears. She smiled weakly at Him as she thought about Him asking her this question when He first came into her garden, *"Will you allow me to move, remove, or prune some things in your garden, Ally? Things that could hurt you or give too much shade to the plants around you, thus causing them not to grow in the Son?"*

She then realized it was pruning time.

❧ DEVOTIONAL GUIDE 33 ❧

"Jesus, I am grateful You told me to practice developing a thankful spirit that helps me focus on You. I can see the difference doing this makes. However, the thought of drastic pruning in the garden of my soul is almost overwhelming. Why do I feel like I might suffocate when I think about this?"

"My love, what you are feeling is not an abnormal reaction, for all who are in the process of learning to trust Me with their most precious inward self often feel this way. Trust is a process that takes time to develop, especially when trust has been so abused by those closest to you. I really do understand. Even many of My closest, trusted disciples did not trust Me when I went to the cross and paid the ultimate price for their salvation.

"During such times of feeling overwhelmed, intentionally focus upon Me. In doing so, remember to not compare Me to those who have abused you or been unkind. I am not like those people. Instead, look at the night skies and realize I made all of this! My written Word says it well,

'Lift up your eyes on high, and see! Who has created these? He Who brings out their host by number and calls them all by name; through the greatness of His might, and because He is strong in power not one is missing or lacks anything' (Isaiah 40:26).

"This army of stars is not made in My image as you are. They do not have My life dwelling in them as you do. My love, focus upon the truth that these stars lack nothing. You, who are My next of kin, will not lack anything in My process of your pruning, healing time. Actually, we will fall more and more in love during the process. Will you take the leap of faith with Me?"

"Yes, I will Jesus."

(Bask in the following Scriptures: 1 Thessalonians 5:18; Isaiah 40:25-31; and Hebrews 2:17-18. Write down your insights.)

My Garden Within

_____

_____

_____

He first walked up to a plant that, to Ally, hadn't seemed that out of shape or overgrown.

Jesus knew her thoughts and responded, "You have to cut back some plants that come up in the spring, and although it sometimes looks worse afterward, it will turn into a beautiful bush." Jesus took the pruning shears and placed them on a branch of the plant.

Ally quickly grabbed His arm. "But Jesus, you are going to cut off the only green on this plant! What will be left?"

"Ally, you need to trust Me." He assured her that He knew what He was doing in her, saying, "We have to cut this to bring the nutrients from the soil; so that they will flow to the other parts of the plant, making it stronger and more beautiful than before." He then snapped off the only green Ally could see on the little bush before her.

Ally gasped and squinted her eyes as it snapped.

"A sharp pruning creates My growth and life in you." He smiled over His shoulder at Ally, who looked a little shocked.

"Think about pruning a tree," He said, stepping toward a tree in her heart. He then looked up through the branches. "We need to climb up there and get rid of the clutter and the dead branches so that the light can reach into it. Sometimes our lives are filled with so much stuff that light, or truth, if you will, cannot penetrate and help us grow."

She loved that He brought Himself to her level with the words *our lives* and *us*. She knew He was right here with her in the process, being Himself formed within her.

"Will you allow Me, your Gardener, to have My way with you so that I can prune and shape you into the woman I created you to be?"

"Cut away, Lord!" Ally grabbed the back of her neck. "Have Your way and prune me and shape me into Your perfected image. Do this so that You can use my life for Your purposes. When others see me, I want them to know that You have shaped me for Yourself, and that You have fashioned me for Your use. Create in me Your life, and use me to reach out to a hurting and dying world."

DEVOTIONAL GUIDE 34

"Jesus, I have chosen to trust You. Please direct my thinking during pruning times when a painful memory engulfs me, and I feel like I am going backward rather than being healed."

Jesus lovingly smiled as He said, "With great delight, I will speak to these times that I understand can be so very frightening, My love. The enemy will use these times to continue to lie to you, telling you I am not present and I do not care. Learn to recognize his lies and as soon as possible say, 'I do not receive! Return to sender!' Replace the lie with My truth that sets you free. Say the truth out loud. Declaring the truth releases power to help in the healing process and the circle of wholeness. Freedom often comes by making you feel miserable first because you are sorting through feelings that have been suppressed for a period of time.

"Also realize what seems to you like moving three steps and falling back two can actually be moving forward. What if it's really five steps forward; and you just didn't think it would feel like you are feeling. Moving forward doesn't always feel good, which we tend to think it should. Feelings can be deceptive. Should you intentionally rebel, stubbornly resist or fall, there will be consequences. You will face the consequences, but My desire is to help you learn from them. However, I won't count it as a failure; you will simply get to do it again. We are revisiting places that are still wounded and bringing healing to these areas. I am the great 'I AM' who is not locked into time and space. I can visit wounded places with you and as you are in My presence I can bring healing. You did not know to let Me be with you when the trauma happened. Now, I can be with you for healing these wounded places. Isn't that good news?

"Whether you feel My presence or not, trust I am there. Give the traumatic memory to Me. Invite Me to tell you what I want you to know about the situation. By faith rest with Me until you are settled within. If needed, use the quiet place where you connect with My presence. My answer may be immediate, or I may wait until another time. Trust with confidence that I am with you."

"Yes, Jesus, I will seek to give You the places I did not know to give in the past that You bring to my mind. Thank You that You will enable me to do so."

(Prayerfully read Romans 10:9-10; Psalms 51:6, 10; 139:23-24; and Psalm 110:1. Jot down your reflections.)

My Garden Within

_____

_____

_____

He continued to cut things off the tree within her. He cut things like insecurity and negativity. He cut off the things that humankind had come up with to add to His message, making it a yoke to enslave instead of the freedom that He intended it to give. He also cut off various lies that she had believed.

It almost looks like this is fun for Him, Ally thought.

Jesus laughed out loud. He said, "I see the finished, flourishing garden, Ally. Do not fear. I do have a plan in this pruning."

He continued to cut—and she felt bitterness fall from her. She felt her unforgiving nature break and fall completely off a memorial plant.

She thought about the fact that He had chosen to leave this plant in her garden to prove that He could turn all things to good for those who love Him, even the hard things that came into her life—that He could use that very thing for Himself so that the world may become whole and healed. By His hand He was perfecting everything that concerned her.

He spoke as He continued to cut on this particular memorial plant. "Again, this was unpleasant to you, but it will bear fruit that you can feed others with, because you have been through it. These are suckers, and if you leave them, they will never bear fruit—they steal energy and nutrients from other parts of the plant." He confirmed her whole thought process.

"I love You, Lord," Ally proclaimed.

Jesus touched Ally's cheek as He walked past her to a cherry tree.

Oh, the love that comes from this Man pierces my heart with one single gaze. I am captivated, she thought.

"We have to cut away branches that have died," Jesus said, and He grunted as the pruning shears came together and a dead branch came crashing down. "Get them out of your garden. Let's cut off all that is not producing fruit and all dead things." He threw aside one of the branches He had just cut.

Ally could see the pile of branches and dead things He was building in her. *Keep going. I feel lighter,* she thought. Her eyes glistened as she looked back to the lover of her soul.

"It takes severe pruning sometimes to bring forth the fruit."

Ally was amazed at the progress Jesus was making in her. He again knew her thoughts.

"It is because you are choosing to stay here with Me, Ally. That is why you can see the progress. As you spend intimate time with Me, I can work on you. Without you abiding in Me here, I could not advance in you like I am."

Amazing, she thought. *Intimate time in the secret place brings ultimate change, not for myself only, but for others also.*

"As you choose to spend time with Me, we will tend to your garden together," He said as He continued to work.

She could see He was working up a sweat.

"It is all so that others may partake of My fruit and therefore become healed and whole themselves."

Ally was finally getting it. "So You will use where the enemy tried to destroy me. You will teach me and heal me; and as I learn from You, I will pour into others' gardens that fertilizer to help them grow?"

Jesus knew she was coming to understand the process.

❧— D E V O T I O N A L   G U I D E   3 5 —❧

"My love, it is important for you to understand that being and staying in My presence is the key to successfully living life and processing pain and trauma. Relationship is the key. The enemy knows this truth and seeks to lure you away from Me.

"It is also important to Me for you to understand My heart is to heal you. I came to set you free from a broken heart and the bondage in which you have been held captive. I ached when your pain happened even more than you have ached with this abuse. I have longed for the time to bring healing and wholeness to you. Now is the time to begin releasing healing!

"As you are healed, not only are you victorious over the evil that was perpetrated upon you, but you gain the authority to lead others in the victory you have acquired. Truly, no pain is wasted as we work together. Victory is gained for My glory and your blessing."

"Thank You, Jesus, for comforting me with Your words and understanding. I choose to process my pain with You, turning it all into resources for Your Kingdom."

(Consider Psalms 147:3; 34:18 and Luke 4:18. Write down what touches your heart.)

My Garden Within

She said, "God has truly caused me to be fruitful in the land of my affliction, that I may feed others through what I've been through."

Jesus could see the tender compassion growing in Ally's heart for others who had walked a hard road. Tender compassion was being birthed in her soul; it was His very heart being formed in her.

Ally looked up through the branches of her well-pruned cherry tree. "Now I can see the light through the branches."

Truth was manifesting in her soul.

Jesus then walked over to a chrysanthemum plant. It had bloomed at one time already, but now all that remained were dead flowers. "If we take off the dead flowers and leaves, Ally, the nutrients of the plant will go to the new buds that are coming. Otherwise, the dead flowers are sucking up the nutrients, trying to live again. Take off the old, useless patterns in your life that have no life in them anyway so that new life may come in their place."

Before Ally's eyes, new mums suddenly budded and bloomed, almost like one of the time-lapse videos she had watched on television.

"There is no time to waste, Ally. Teach what you do know already. Feed with the fruit I am forming in you. Trust Me. I am with you." Jesus then approached her until they were face to face.

"All authority in heaven and on earth has been given to Me. Go, then, with Me, and give what you've been given. Teach all that you have been taught, and encourage those you teach to do the same. I am with you all your days. I am with you always, and I continue with you without interruption. Believe that, Ally, on every occasion I am with you. We are one now. Abide in Me, and I will abide in you always."

Ally was overwhelmed with the great commission Jesus had bestowed upon her. She realized that this life was not just about her and that there was a bigger and more majestic picture. Jesus wanted no soul she knew to perish—He wanted all to know Him as she did. Now she knew she had work to do: to plant and live His life, to restore with and for Him, to speak, to go.

Jesus smiled at her with tears in His eyes. She was receiving His very heart into her own. He began to sing, and His voice was sweet to Ally's ears.

> *I am in My vineyard, My vineyard beloved and lovely.*
> *I the Lord am its Keeper, this vineyard beloved and lovely.*
> *I water it every moment. Lest anyone harm it,*
> *I guard and I keep it night and day.*
> *Take root, My garden. Take root,*
> *My vineyard. Blossom for Me.*
> *Open up for Me.*
> *Take root, My garden. Send forth your shoots.*
> *Fill the whole world with fruit,*
> *the fruit of knowing Me,*
> *The one true God who watches over you.*
> *You are My beloved.*
> *You are My vineyard. You are My garden.*
> *You are My bride.*

His song came to her as her life's new song.

It's all about Him now—about Him and for Him, she thought.

Ally was beginning to see His life forming in her, even though she had a ways to go on this journey. She looked toward the pile of branches that Jesus had cut out of her life, and amazingly before her eyes they burst into flames!

She remembered reading in her Bible, in John 15, about branches being thrown into the fire and burned—all dead and useless things burned. They burned up very quickly, and there she was, standing in front of a pile of ashes. She felt the need to dig in them, and as she did, there in the center of them was an ordinary, brown stone. As she continued to look at it, it began to look different; there were little gold specks shining out of it.

Jesus spoke to her soul. "The Gardener brings the change. You just have to look for it, and, better yet, expect it. I will bring beauty out of the ashes," He said.

DEVOTIONAL GUIDE 36

"My love, you may be encouraged to read about others' struggle to move from being survivors to thriving with Me. I offered the Israelites the Promised Land where they could thrive. When they viewed the land, they saw only themselves as grasshoppers and the people as giants stronger than they were. Caleb, one of the twelve men sent to spy out the land, saw with eternal eyes, seeing nothing is impossible when you walk with God.

"So, My love, I ask you to learn two things from My people as recorded in My Word. Magnify Me as a way of life. Magnifying Me will enlarge Me in your eyes as to who I am what I can do and want to do. Everything is easy for Me. I simply desire your agreement and cooperation.

"Next, keep in mind the maturing process is 'little by little.' Listen to My words to the Israelites in Exodus 23:29-30: *'I will not drive them out from before you in one year, lest the land become desolate [for lack of attention] and the wild beasts multiply against you. Little by little I will drive them out from before you, until you have increased and are numerous enough to take possession of the land.'*

"When you learn a truth, you need to embrace it, walk in it, and stand resisting the enemy thereby making it truly part of you. It takes time to learn, assimilate, and establish. This is the reason you must take your personal land/garden gradually, as the Israelites were encouraged to do. This is the way you possess your inward land of your soul, moving into maturity and wholeness."

"Jesus, thank You so much for these insights. I will start practicing magnifying You by thanking You for the good things I see and by reading about the miracles You did in Your Word and around me. I am beginning to have new hope for my future."

(Carefully read the following Scriptures asking the Holy Spirit to show you what He wants you to see: Numbers 13:27-33; Exodus 23:29-30; and Psalm 69:30. Write down your thoughts and review them until they are settled in your heart.)

My Garden Within

She added the rock to the rest, and then she closed her eyes and prayed. "God, I understand that the most important thing I can do as You prune me is to yield to You. I am done with the things in my life that keep me unfruitful. I am finished being my own gardener of my soul, and so I give You the shears. You know what is best for me. Here," she said, grabbing the shears that were now lying close by and held them up to Jesus, "please do what You need to do. I want Your Holy Spirit to flow through me in all that I do and say. And I ask You to put Your desires into my heart. I want Your very heart to beat inside of mine. I want the heart of our Father. Let the fruit that is produced in my garden be an extension of You and Your love. I pray that Your peace, goodness, and faithfulness would be fashioned in me. Let Your gentleness be evident in me and Your fruit of self-control be noticeable in my life. Jesus, I need

You. Without You and apart from You, there is no life. You are the vine, and I am the branch. Be my Master Gardener. In Jesus' name, amen."

Ally opened her eyes to find herself once again in her big leather chair, the fire before her flickering. It seemed as if the fire itself was smiling and delighted by her.

Oh, the presence of God. There is none like You.

My Garden Within

Devotional Guide Inventory Chapter 8

1. Have you ever felt overwhelmed or as if you were suffocating from problems from the past or now? How can you overcome such feelings? What is the process of developing trust? Does Jesus understand?

2. Can processing painful memories or present pain make you feel like you are moving backward rather than forward? What do you do when the enemy tells you Jesus has forsaken you or doesn't care? What does Jesus being the Great "I AM" really mean? How do you get Jesus' insight for your painful experiences?

3. What is the key to successfully processing not only life but also pain? What is Jesus' heart toward your pain? When you are healed, how will this be used positively for the Kingdom of God?

4. What biblical example shows a group of people's failure to thrive? How can we not repeat this tragic situation?

5. Why does God most often bring healing "little by little"? Does this principle also apply to you? Why?

My Garden Within Inventory

_____

_____

_____

_____

_____

_____

_____

_____

_____

_____

_____

_____

_____

_____

_____

_____

_____

_____

_____

_____

_____

_____

_____

_____

CHAPTER 9

Come for a Swim

He who believes in Me [who cleaves to and trusts in and relies on Me] as the Scripture has said, from his innermost being shall flow [continuously] springs and rivers of living water (John 7:38).

The next day Ally was out deadheading flowers in her garden at home. She was trying to remember everything that Jesus had taught her the day before. She remembered a Scripture she had recently read that said that the Holy Spirit, the very Spirit of Jesus Himself, would remind her and bring to her remembrance everything that Jesus had told her.

"Holy Spirit, come" were the next words out of her mouth. She then heard Jesus' sweet voice.

"Come for a swim," He said.

Ally went over to a wooden bench in her yard and sat down. She looked up toward heaven, and she began to hear the sound of rushing water. Before she knew it, she was beholding a great waterfall and the clear and sparkling river below it. She was before the river in her garden.

"This is the living water that waters your garden!" Jesus yelled down from the top of this great waterfall in Ally's garden.

She smiled up at Him.

"It comes from Eden to water your garden!" He shouted to her as He began His descent to meet with her.

How quickly He moves down this mountain, she thought. *Behold, He comes, leaping upon the mountains, bounding over the hills, to meet with me. Oh heart, do not come out of my chest, for I feel you may burst with love for this Man!*

Before she was aware of what was happening, Jesus had captured her heart with His amazing love and dove with her into the deep. Her body was submerged in the living water. Instead of being terrified by the deep water, she felt a sense of being completely covered in Him and kept by Him. She knew that He had grasped her heart and that He would not let her drown. Amazingly, she could still breathe. She felt a deep yearning to stay under this water, for in it she was being filled with the very Spirit of God. Life. This was the River of Life itself. Life was filling every abandoned hole in her life. Every hurt, every lie, and every bit of hopelessness was being filled with this living water. This water was alive.

As they surfaced, Jesus laughed. He loved to wash His beloved ones with the Water of Life. He knew the Holy Spirit had filled Ally with God's very life. He turned to her, and with His hands He brushed her hair out of her face and wiped the water off her cheeks.

DEVOTIONAL GUIDE 37

"Jesus, I felt so blessed looking at my beautiful double red poppies blooming in my flower garden outside my screen porch this morning. You know how I have worked for these in a different part of my garden. Now I realize they are in a strategic place, better than I would have ever planned, but so different. I planted and worked hard for what seemed good, but then it didn't happen as I planned. Something better happened. Help me to wrap my mind around this process."

"My love, thank you for asking Me to explain. The Kingdom of God is coming forth from within you, the garden of your soul. It is so different from the world in which you are accustomed to living. It is a new way of thinking, relating, and living. In this Kingdom you learn who I am and who you are. We both have identities. When you live according to your identity (your real self) in My resurrection power, nothing can shake you, cause you to lose your footing, or steal your peace as a way of life.

"In My Word in Exodus 3:14, I told Moses, '*I AM WHO I AM AND WHAT I AM, and I WILL BE WHAT I WILL BE....*' As your spirit is strengthened by My truth, your human spirit will lead from within. The soul will learn to stop surviving and submit to your human spirit. The thriving reconciliation that happens will provide the stability necessary to let My peace rule as a way of life. You are learning to trust Me and let Me be in control.

"When you recognized and rejoiced over where your poppies were blooming rather than grumbling and fretting because they were not where you planted them, we made giant steps toward establishing the identity I have for you. The attitude of flowing with the living water I am releasing within, even though you don't know what will happen next, is big steps forward. You trusted what I am doing, knowing it is good. You are choosing to be filled and stimulated with the (Holy) Spirit as My Word directs in Ephesians 5:18. You are cooperating with Me, trusting Me to be in control. It is about who you allow to be in control—you or Me. Be encouraged, My love, you are moving forward."

"Jesus, I choose Your control. I am beginning to realize that turning my control over to You and embracing Your control is so major. Holy Spirit, please convict me every time I grieve You by not yielding to You. Thank You for helping me."

(Meditate upon the following Scriptures: Luke 17:21; Exodus 3:14; and Ephesians 5:18,30. Record your observations.)

My Garden Within

---

"For whoever believes in Me, who cleaves to, trusts in, and relies on Me from his or her innermost being as the Scripture has said, shall flow continuously springs and rivers of living water, just like this." He was speaking here of the Spirit of God filling her.

"With much joy you will draw water from this river, Ally. This life, this salvation from the Holy Spirit, of which this water is a symbol of—you need to draw it up out of yourself to water both yourself and others with it."

Jesus cupped His hands and pulled some water up with them, letting it fall slowly back into the river.

"You see, Ally, without water you would die. You need to water daily with the water of the Word. Don't waste your time watering with the world. If you take the l out of world, it becomes Word. Cut off the l, the lusts of the flesh, the lusts of the eyes, laziness, and lies. Those things bring a life-threatening drought to your garden. Lies are a false statement or belief deliberately presented as being true, and if you don't have the truth in you, you will begin to believe those lies. Wash yourself daily with truth, My truth. Take a swim daily in life and in this river. Submerge yourself in Me. I have ransomed you, Ally, and redeemed you from the enemy of your soul. Your life is now going to be like a well-watered garden—full of beauty and fullness, bearing much fruit, life-giving, and nourishing. But you need to water. You need to spend time tending the garden of your soul."

Why would I want to be anywhere else? I am loved completely here, she thought.

"Praise and worship also effectively water the seeds that you plant and your existing plants." He wrung the water from His hair. "I want to enjoy you. Do you know that is why you were created? For My pleasure. I delight in you, and I love you tremendously."

# DEVOTIONAL GUIDE 38

"Jesus, I want to eliminate the life-threatening drought in my garden caused by the lies I have believed and the various lusts I have fed. I thank You that You have redeemed my life from the enemy of my soul. Help me to know how to cooperate with You."

With excitement Jesus said, "The Word, which is Me, became flesh—full of grace and truth. And of His fullness we have all received, and grace for grace, according to John 1:14, 16. My love, you are graciously receiving the truth I am showing you about yourself and your identity. Realize My grace is your resource and inheritance to receive My living water, but My grace is given to you also to release this truth and life to others. Grace really means you have My unchanging favor, My resurrection power, and My nature poured out on your behalf. You have all that is needed to accomplish everything I ask you to do and be without apology. My grace can never be exhausted. It is based on My nature, not your failures or successes. Just as a tree simply receives the sunshine, rain, and nutrients from the ground, open your receiver in your heart and soak in My grace. It cannot be earned only accepted."

"Wow, that seems too good to be true, Jesus!"

"That's Kingdom living in the garden of your soul, My love. As you receive and cooperate together with Me, the works that the enemy has done in your soul are abolished. That is why I came. Let Me remind you, My elect, that I not only delight in you, but also listen to what I say in Zephaniah 3:17: *'He will rejoice over you with joy; He will rest [in silent satisfaction] and in His love He will be silent and make no mention [of past sins, or even recall them]; He will exult over you with singing.'* My love that is Me talking about you! Receive my grace poured out to you."

"Yes, Jesus. I will read these passages over and over until my heart knows they are true. I love You."

(Bask in John 1:14, 16; 2 Corinthians 9:8; Isaiah 42:1; Zephaniah 3:17. Jot down your thoughts.)

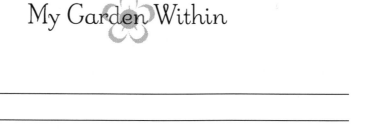

My Garden Within

As He spoke those words, He playfully dunked Ally in the water and then joyfully laughed, pulling her up onto the riverbank. He continued to captivate her heart as He spoke, saying, "When the world comes in and tries to take My place in your heart, keep your confidence and hope in Me. For if you do this, you will be like a tree planted by this living water, that spreads its roots by this river. You shall not fear when heat comes, for your leaves will stay green. You will not be anxious and full of care in the year of drought, nor will you cease yielding fruit."

Ally looked around and saw many trees planted by the river.

"Soak yourself in Me, Ally, because mere surface sprinkling encourages shallow roots, which are vulnerable to scorching in the hot sun. When circumstances and storms in life come up, plants can die because they are not rooted deeply enough." He pulled a wilted plant from the soil in her heart, and its root was only an inch long. "My love is enough. I am love. I am your *enough.*" He reached down and moved His hand against the current of the river, saying, "This water is My Holy Spirit, and He will teach you all things, and you will be filled and give this life-giving water to others. I will water you every moment, and I promise you that if you water others, you yourself will be watered."

Ally had not spoken in all this time; she was just trying to take it all in—to let it soak in, so to speak. "I so want to let You flow out of me continuously, but I feel like I just don't know enough yet," she said, hanging her head.

Immediately, Jesus lifted her chin up with His right hand. "You see, that is the biggest lie in My family right now. You need to meditate on what you *do* know! Pour out your life and the water you do have on others. Give them a taste of the living water you do have, and you will realize that it continues to flow out of you in fullness. You see, it has nothing to do with you and everything to do with Me."

He pointed to Ally's heart. "I live here in you, and I *am* that fullness."

Ally thought, *Truth. He speaks the truth that sets me free.*

"The enemy of your soul will try to stop the flow of My Spirit in you by filling you with dirt, which are those lies. The world or your own thoughts will try to stop up your well of living water. But don't stop digging it out. Seek truth, and seek Me. I am your salvation, and I will save you from the world. You see, I have already overcome it, so be of good cheer," He said with a smile. "But again, you have to choose—choose to dig until you find water, for My springs are always there. Then with joy you will draw My water out of your life to give life wherever you go."

They stood together, and as they turned, a three-tiered fountain appeared in the midst of her garden. This fountain was larger and more glorious than any fountain she had ever seen before. It had intricate designs carved into it of almond flowers, grape vines, birds, and fruit.

Just beautiful. Astonishing, she thought.

Jesus said, "This is the fountain of skillful and godly wisdom, and it flows like a gushing stream. Its waters are sparkling, fresh, pure, and life-giving. It is here for you, in you."

DEVOTIONAL GUIDE 39

"I want skillful and godly wisdom, Jesus. How is wisdom and character bringing forth my identity in You developed?"

"You, My love, have the major role in your character building. Character cannot be inherited. You are in a moral workshop determining if you grow to your full potential while living in time and space. Only through individual free choice is godly character possible. Each time you say no to temptation, you grow in godly character. Character doesn't have to do with environment, but rather with the choices you make.

"Adam and Eve lived in a perfect environment but made the wrong choice. Character comes with the exercise of the will in regard to moral choices. The exercise of making a value judgment brings about an understanding of good and evil. If Adam and Eve had said 'No' to the temptation to eat of the tree of good and evil, they would have experienced a brief glimpse into the moral realm (good and evil). With each successive victory they would have grown in righteousness. Every time they said 'No' to eating of the tree, they would have been more confirmed in righteousness. It would have resulted in the development of character. They would have known evil from afar, while they would have known righteousness intimately.

"Your soul is your sacred ground. I can rebuke a storm at sea, reshape the earth or the heavens by My Word, but I want a Bride who makes the choice to be molded into My image and to partner with Me. I am a gentleman, not a bully. When your heart is set upon righteous choices, I have the glory for which I gladly suffered to have you by My side for now and eternity. As we work together, My Kingdom not only comes within you but also flows out to others."

"Oh, Jesus, I want to lay my life down to give You the reward of Your suffering. I want to apply every drop of the blood You shed for me to heal my wounds, to meet my needs, and unravel my issues thereby having the victory You purchased on the cross in order that Your image is reflected within me."

(Study Genesis 2:15-17; 3:1-6 and 1 Corinthians 10:13-14. Write your commitment.)

My Garden Within

_____

_____

_____

Ally put her hand into the stream of water as it poured from one tier to another. "I want people to drink of You when they are around me."

"They will, if you draw Me out. I will be that life-giving drink to them as you stir Me up within yourself. You shall be like the pool of Bethesda to the world. Just as the one was healed as My Spirit stirred the waters of that pool, I will stir you to bring life-giving water wherever you go, to bring Me wherever you go. Life will flourish wherever this water flows."

Ally remembered the story in the Bible of the man healed in a pool, and the place was called Bethesda.

"This living water is the Holy Spirit flowing out of you continuously, as the Scripture has said. That is My heart for you, Ally. Draw deep into this water. Give My life-drink to those around you, because once they drink of Me, their thirst for the things of the world will diminish. Their wilderness and dry land will be glad and watered, and they will live again. With joy, Ally, give this water out."

Jesus cupped His hands under the flowing water until they were filled and drank from the water in His hands.

"Some of My chosen ones are in the desert right now where there is no water, and without water they will die. The waters that I want to have flow through them are dormant and inactive. Those waters in them are latent, but they are capable of being active. They are in a relatively inactive condition, and because of that, some of my processes that I have planned for them are slowed down or even suspended."

Ally thought of Old Faithful, the geyser at Yellowstone Park, and the fact that its period of activity was spaced far apart. She realized that the Lord's plan was for everyone to flow continuously.

She again saw a tear making its way down Jesus' face.

"Will you be My oasis, Ally? In their desert? Will you be a presence of water, My water?"

"What exactly is an oasis?" she asked.

"An oasis is a small place preserved from surrounding unpleasantness. It is a green area in the desert. It is a place that provides refuge and relief," He answered.

Ally began to realize that this was part of her destiny in Him—to be this place or oasis for others.

"So many of Mine are in that place and surrounded by unpleasantness. I long to give them a drink, to take them for a swim in My life, My river, like I did with you." He wiped His tear. "If they would just come to Me. Will you bring Me to them, Ally? Will you go? Only My water will refresh, support, and strengthen their souls."

With that said, Ally suddenly found herself in a boat on a pond inside her soul, in her garden. She was lying in the boat with her arms over the side, playfully running them through the water. *What peace and what life*, she thought.

She glanced at her reflection in the water, and suddenly the face of Jesus filled the pond. It was then she saw them coming; for miles she could see people coming to the waters.

"They are coming for Me," Ally heard from within. "Give them a drink."

Ally cupped her hands and lifted some of the water from the pond. The water looked alive because it was moving in her palm. It then took the form of her next stone—blue, brilliant, life-giving water. She looked up at the multitudes and just smiled; she knew she had life within her—His life, for them.

DEVOTIONAL GUIDE 40

"Jesus, it is easy for me to share with those I like and feel we have a lot of things in common. How can I love those who are repulsive to me or those I simply do not like? Please give me insight as to how to cooperate with You in loving those who I don't naturally like."

Jesus smiled with delight. He said, "My love, this is true Kingdom living, which is not only allowing the garden of your soul to be restored, but also expanding your Garden of Eden to the rest of the world. Remember how I used others to give you hope and to know My love? Take a while and remember. Now, realize I was using the people and situations you remember to draw you to Myself. You were and are learning to be fully alive in Me. My heart is made up of all My next of kin. I am not satisfied until My entire family is fully alive in Me. Using eternal eyes, see My potential in the people with whom you do not identify. Know they are made in My image just as you are. I love them as I love you.

"Reach out to them as if you were reaching out to Me, because you are. As you love them unconditionally and accept them where they are, I will use you as a conduit or vessel through which My drawing love flows. Will you do this for Me?

"An exciting feature of the assignment, My love, is you just might find yourself loving those I love. We will eventually enjoy a huge circle of love. A group hug! A divine love-in!"

"Yes, Jesus, that is a plan I will embrace. I love learning to love You in many different ways."

(Ponder the following Scriptures: Mark 12:30-31; Matthew 25:34-40; and 1 Corinthians 10:31. Process before Him the thoughts you have written down.)

My Garden Within

_____

_____

_____

Devotional Guide Inventory Chapter 9

1. How have you responded in the past when things didn't go as you planned? How do you see that God wants you to respond? Is releasing your control of the situation scary or a relief? How is this allowing the Kingdom of God to expand through you and in you?

2. What has grace meant to you in the past? What really is God's grace? Can you earn, deserve, or do anything to increase His grace? What is your part in cooperating with His grace? Do you have all the grace you need to fulfill your destiny?

3. Who plays the major role in developing your character? How is character developed? How did Adam and Eve sabotage their character development? Will Jesus force you to make the right decisions? Do you have provided for you the necessary resources to make godly decisions producing divine character?

4. Who does Jesus want to use to expand His Kingdom? How can you love those you don't like? What is the end result when you do it His way?

My Garden Within Inventory

_____

_____

_____

_____

_____

_____

_____

_____

_____

_____

_____

_____

_____

_____

_____

_____

_____

_____

_____

CHAPTER 10

Weeds

Exuberant and passionate thinking. This is the glorious life of the mind enlisted in the service of God.

I'll transform her dead ground into Eden, her moonscape into the garden of God, a place filled with exuberance and laughter, thankful voices and melodic songs (Isaiah 51:3 The Message Remix[1]).

Ally decided to venture back to the entrance of her garden, back to the place where she first saw the condition of her heart, and to her surprise it looked exactly the same. She frowned as she scanned the sad scenery surrounding her. She looked to the ground, where she had previously uncovered the little green shoot. It was still there, trying to smile at her but feeling very intimidated by the weeds still surrounding it.

"New weeds come daily," she heard Jesus say.

She looked around but couldn't see Him.

"Therefore, weeding is a daily job," He said. His voice was coming from above her.

She looked up, and there He was, sitting on her garden wall. In His mouth was the shaft of a wheat stalk. He was chewing on the end.

"You kind of look like a farmer," Ally said as she giggled.

"That's the look I was aiming for," He said and smiled. He jumped down from His high place in her. "It looks like these weeds are suffocating our little friend here."

He bent down and pulled a few weeds to make room for this tiny plant to breathe. "Beware, Ally, of quick-growing weeds that try to spring up because of circumstances in your life. They will accumulate and try to destroy your garden."

He motioned for her to help Him.

"If you don't deal with these circumstances or problems in your life, they have a way of growing like these weeds here. And if you give them complete access to grow in your mind, these problems could become your lifestyle, and that lifestyle will suffocate all the good things that we have planted. If that life reigns, My life in you won't."

He bit His bottom lip, looked around her soul, and continued. "It's not enough to just love this garden life, Ally; you have to hate the weeds that try to choke the life from it."

Ally thought about that statement. *I hate the weeds I see choking the life from those around me—or choking me, myself. We have to hate the destroyer of life, peace, and joy. We need to despise those things that steal or choke our garden life, those things in life that sneak in and steal our time or joy.*

Jesus then said, "Weeds suffocate life; that is their job, and they are good at it. I have to teach you to recognize them. Then root out, pull up, and kill those weeds every day so that you can truly live. Freely live. As I said, weeding is a daily job, and sometimes a minute-by-minute job. You see, things like being offended plant a weed seed inside you, and if you don't deal with it, it will grow and become difficult to pull up later. All that the enemy needs to do is drop one of his little seeds in your heart or mind, and then he walks away. It's your choice whether you water that seed or not."

He came to a hearty weed that was planted in her heart. "Try to pull this one up," He said, pointing to it. Even at His pointing finger, the weed began to quiver.

Ally walked over to this haughty weed and grasped the base of it; although she pulled with all her might, the weed didn't budge.

"If you would have pulled this up when it was first planted in you, it would have been much easier, because the roots wouldn't have been deep yet."

Ally took a deep breath.

"If you remain in Me and walk with Me, I will point out the beginning of weeds. I see them. And if we pull them up when they are small, that is much easier than trying to pull larger weeds like this one."

DEVOTIONAL GUIDE 41

"Jesus, I am beginning to realize that only You can turn my desolate moonscape garden areas into Eden. I have such huge damaged places because I have pushed down, suppressed, and denied many weeds for so long. Now I cannot keep them hidden any longer. What do I do? What has happened? I want You to reign in my life, not my past circumstances or these ugly weeds."

"My special treasured one, I have waited for this time to begin a deep healing within you. I never wanted you to be traumatized or wounded. To have a Bride, who has a choice, has meant many would choose evil and not My way, thereby hurting themselves and others. I experienced the depth of the horrendous evil done to you while on the cross. It was covered by My life-healing blood. I have continued to intercede for you until healing could be brought to your emotions," Jesus said. "Now, is the time to let the healing begin!

"Your emotions held the major part of the pain until now, allowing the rest of your soul to survive. Now it is time for your emotions, which were blocked off or fragmented, to be released and healed. The process may seem long to you, but it often takes time to restore damage that has been so devastating. Change often needs to be gradual so more traumas are not induced. This time will be used to not only give you freedom, but it will also give you the needed authority to take others through the same freeing process that you have traveled.

"First, let's reassure your emotions that we will not leave them while the stored up pain is being released. To do that you, My special treasure, you need to stay in My presence, which is the only place pain is successfully processed. Commit to staying in My presence even when you don't feel I am here. Choose to believe the truth that I will never, ever forsake you. When the painful memories come, run to Me. By agreeing and cooperating with Me, we enjoy a life-changing partnership. This is your strategic part. Go to your quiet place until your soul is settled if needed in order to return the healing process.

"Next, tell your emotions you appreciate their holding this pain all this time. Reassure your emotions they have been very brave and strong. You are so proud of them. You are looking forward to their being free to love without fear or self-protection.

"Ask your emotions to open the door to the prison where the pain has been held for so long allowing Me to bring comfort and reassurance that I am here to restore. The latch to your emotions is yours to control from within. I am not a bully. I will do nothing without your consent. Your trauma came because your right to choose was violated. You experienced things you didn't want and I didn't want for you. Give Me permission to show your emotions My loving heart."

"Yes, Jesus, I trust You because You gave Your life that I may have life. Release Your love into my emotions. You know best!"

(Carefully and prayerfully read Isaiah 61, Romans 8:26-34, and James 4:8. Record what speaks to you.)

My Garden Within

_____

_____

_____

Ally tried again by herself to pull up that stubborn weed. "I remember," she started, "when I had my first garden at home. I didn't always stay up on the weeding process. When I did, they were few and easy to pull, because they were small. But it seemed that even a few days would go by, and if I didn't tend my garden, I'd go out and *bam*—a ton of weeds!"

She again tugged with all her might at this huge weed in her soul and said, "I remember one that got so big, like this one, that I couldn't pull it by myself. The roots were too strong, and I needed someone stronger than me to pull it up."

Jesus replied, "Sometimes you need to find someone to pray with you in agreement to remove these obstinate weeds—maybe one who has walked with Me through something similar and because of that has become a little stronger than you. You see, I made My people to need one another and to help one another—just like I will use you to help pull up some things in other people's gardens."

Ally pushed her hair from her face. She had begun to sweat, trying to pull up this booger of a weed. "This big weed in my garden at home," she continued, though she was out of breath as she wiped some sweat from her brow. "There was no one around I could find to help, so I took a hose."

She then grabbed a hose that was lying nearby that was being fed water from the River of Life in her. "And I ran water on this massive weed until the soil beneath it became mud. It took awhile for the water to get deep enough, but that made pulling it out by the root easier."

She continued watering at the base of this weed in her soul. "And I got this revelation from You, Lord, I believe," she said, smiling up at Him. "That the water of Your Word, Your truth, softens the ground of my heart and loosens every wrongful thing planted there."

With that said, and with the water still running, she again yanked on this awful plant, and it came out of her, roots and all. As it did, she fell on her backside because she was yanking so hard.

Jesus began laughing. "I love when you get it," He said, reaching out His hand to help her up. "My truth will set you free!"

Ally felt a sense of freedom in her that she had not felt in a long time. He lifted her up.

"It's gone," she said and smiled. "The bad feelings inside and the sorrow are all gone." She looked to the weed she had pulled out with truth. "Look at the size of that root!" she exclaimed. "No wonder it had remained in me for so long." She began to laugh and just couldn't stop until tears were running down her cheeks. "Thank You, Jesus."

The weed before her already had begun to wilt. The thing that had been so stately on the inside of her for so long and refused to surrender, now just lay as a sad clump before her eyes. It was no longer imposing and no longer powerful.

"If you keep your mind and your thoughts on Me, I will kill the things that have tried to rule your life, the things that suffocate My life in you—like this weed here," He proclaimed, picking up the weed that Ally had just pulled from her heart. "This former tyrant master is dead. It shall not live or reappear, because you got the root lie out. It is now a powerless ghost. It shall not rise or come back again."

He then looked directly at the weed and said, "I will cause every memory and every trace of your so-called supremacy over this life to perish!" He threw the weed over the wall, and it was now totally out of her garden. "There is a war with weeds until I come and conquer them and until I replace them with Myself, and with My truth, through your surrender."

Truth had filled the hole left by that ugly weed.

DEVOTIONAL GUIDE 42

"Jesus, I love learning to trust You, but some of my big weeds or traumas, are so horrific I get lost in the past chaotic memory. How do I navigate this land mine of pain?"

Jesus was pleased to answer. With an affectionate, compassionate smile He said, "You must choose to stay in My presence, which is the first step, but I am so pleased when My Body works together to help each other. Seek out a mature mentor who will pray with you and counsel you during the confusing time of sorting out the precious from the vile. It is hard to be objective about yourself. People either think too highly or too destructively about themselves. Each is pride with opposite manifestations. One says I need no help and the other tries to draw his or her help from another instead of Me.

"Either through a prayer time with your mentor or through counseling to sort out what is happening, your healing can be hastened. Ask Me to bring a mature Christian mentor or counselor to you or seek one out via your pastor. As you work together, you will both learn and grow in Me. We share the treasure hunt together discovering who He created you to be and how you reflect My image. I have placed priceless treasures within you which will be exciting to discover and enjoy. Each enjoys Kingdom Body life, bringing My Kingdom to earth one by one."

"Jesus, I am comforted to know how You lead. I choose Your way. I will seek Your direction for a mentor to help me weed my garden."

(Study the following Scriptures asking the Holy Spirit to open your eyes to His direction: Proverbs 11:14; 12:15; 19:20; 24:6; 27:9; 1 Corinthians 12:12-18; and James 5:16. Write down what you glean.)

My Garden Within

Get to the Root

With this stronghold out of her life, Ally began pulling up the smaller weeds in her heart with ease. She had a new hope and new strength. Both she and Jesus were sitting in the midst of these surrounding weeds, and most of them took on the form of dandelions.

"You know how that weed finally came out, root and all?" Jesus asked. "If we pull the weeds but the roots remain, it will just allow that same weed to pop back up again."

As Jesus spoke, Ally pulled on a dandelion and heard that popping sound. "Oh, that is not good," she said. "That sound means that even though it looks like the weed is gone, the root remains embedded in the ground."

The next one she pulled came out roots and all. "Victory!" she shouted.

Jesus smiled in response to her victory shout.

Ally remembered mowing her lawn at her home, which had quite a few dandelions growing in it. Normally she just mowed them down because that was easier than pulling them out, and for a while, it looked like all was well. But they did come back, and they came back worse than before.

"Why, sometimes, do we try what we think is the easy way, Jesus?"

He had just taken the top off a weed and left the root, pointing to it. "Because they do seem gone, for a while, and it is easier to just snap the top off. But easy isn't always the best answer."

He dug a little deeper and pulled out the root He had just left. "Disciplining your thoughts, for instance, is hard work. Some people try to control their mouths, but they do nothing about their thoughts. That is like pulling off the top of a weed. Unless the root is dug up, the weeds always come back." He threw the root off to the side.

"Also, excuses, such as those for behaving badly, are like weeds. If left unattended they will choke the fruit, or life, in you. Self-pity, envy, an unforgiving heart, bitterness, anger—all those will grow like bad weeds and choke what I am doing and want to do in your life." He looked around at the existing weeds.

Ally sighed and said, "This is hard work."

"But look how much we've done in just a short time already," He replied. He glanced around her heart and added, "But yes, it is hard work. But it will yield a harvest of righteousness and blessing as you continue. Continue with Me, and we will kindly pull up all these weeds!"

He pointed His finger toward the remaining weeds in her garden. "Make Me your habit, Ally. Daily you need to choose Me, to choose life, over and over and over again, until that becomes your habit. Imagine that!" He grinned. "A habit of joy, truth, abundant life, and peace."

Ally thought about the meaning of the word *habit.*

Jesus, knowing this, answered, "A habit is a constant, sometimes unconscious inclination to perform an act, and it is formed or acquired through its frequent repetition. You do it and do it and do it again."

"I want You to be my habit, Jesus," Ally replied.

"Then remain in Me, walk with Me daily, and let Me be your constant companion. You see, you are either walking with Me, in My presence, or you are walking in the flesh, which is your own way of thinking and doing. Like I said before, you don't have to work at being in the flesh. You don't work to plant weeds."

She looked to her feet, where weeds were still surrounding her. "Nope, I surely didn't plant these."

"Here is how I become your habit, Ally. Are you ready for this?"

He had her complete focus.

DEVOTIONAL GUIDE 43

"Jesus, I have felt such shame, guilt, and worthlessness for so long it has become a habit to think of myself that way. I know others abused me without my consent and projected upon me the lies I have embraced. I do not want to make excuses anymore; I want to assume responsibility for my life from now on cooperating with You to replace the lies with truth. How do I lay down the evil of the past?"

Jesus was eager to share how to be the real person He saw and created before the foundation of the world and still sees buried under the wounded emotions. With a twinkle in His eyes indicating how delighted He was to be with me, He said, "My special treasure, old habits are hard to break, but since I have already broken them for you on the cross, as we walk together we empty the trenches filled with lies, wounds, and unmet needs with My life and My truth. In this process you learn to fall more deeply in love with Me. The strategy is simple but takes concentrated hard work that pays divine dividends for now and eternity.

"Look at yourself in the mirror, eye to eye, and speak to yourself My truth each morning and evening. In this way, you methodically take off or strip off the ill-fitting, filthy clothes of the past. Lay them at the foot of the cross. See My life-cleansing blood cover them. Then speak the truth to yourself, which is what I say in My Word about you.

"For instance, when the enemy not only says you are shameful but will also remain shameful, you speak to him the truth. This is the way we undo his evil works. You quote My Words written down which say, I am *'a living stone, rejected indeed by men, but chosen by God and precious... [a] living stone being built up a spiritual house...who believes on Him will by no means be put to shame'* (1 Peter 2:4-6 NKJV). I now take off shame and say for you to go be the footstool of Jesus. Now I put on my new garment of righteousness because I am in Jesus.

"Say this to yourself every time the old garments rise up, replacing them with the new clothing. It takes time. Don't be discouraged. These are your character-building, discipline exercises and choices that partner with My resurrection life-changing power."

"Jesus, I am going to make little cards with Your truth written so I can remember to speak the truth to myself as a way of life. Once it is established, I will make a new card speaking to the next lie I have believed."

(Ponder the following Scriptures: Ephesians 4:22-32; Colossians 3:1-10; 2 Corinthians 5:21; and 1 Peter 2:4-8. Record your reflections.)

My Garden Within

"Relate all of your life to God, to Me, our Father, and the Holy Spirit. Everything. Connect everything to God. Talk to Us. Interact with Us. Work with Us so that we can carry Our purpose for you in the world to its completion."

Ally was trying to really grasp what He was saying.

"Live in Our companionship, Ally. Companionship comes from the word *company.*"

Ally thought about the times when she invited company over. She smiled when she thought, *I'm having God over tonight.*

"Live in the company of God; live in Our presence continuously. Spend time with Us, Ally."

A little finch landed on the wall above their heads and sang out a little song. "Again, relate all of your life to Us. Everything in your life, Ally—see it through Our eyes and through Our perspective. You see, you have a different perspective from down here, which basically means you have a different view. We know what we are doing, Ally. Ask for Our perspective."

Ally thought about how earlier that week she was in a crowd of people when she noticed a little girl pulling on her daddy's pant leg. "Lift me up, Daddy," the little girl had exclaimed. "I can't see from down here."

Wow, she thought, and then she looked at Jesus and said, "Pick me up, Jesus. I also cannot see from down here."

Jesus knew she was grasping His truth.

"Get Our thoughts on every situation." He continued, "Get Our perspective, Our guidance. Ask Me what I say or think about every situation."

He glanced around her heart. "Keep alert, Al. Watch for weeds, and be sensitive about what is going on in and around you. Be attentive to your garden life but also to the gardens surrounding you." He was speaking of other people in her life.

"Always ask yourself this question, as it will help you in life: 'Does this affect my intimacy with God?' That will help you to choose life and to live on purpose. You know, when you fully comprehend that there is more to life than just the here and now, and you realize that this life is just a training ground for eternity spent with Me, you will begin to live differently. That is Our perspective, Ally."

He spread His hands out wide. "You will begin to live in the reality of eternity, right here and now; and that will affect how you handle everything. Every relationship, task, situation, and circumstance. To make the most out of your life, keep the picture of eternity continuously in your mind, in your heart, and in your garden."

DEVOTIONAL GUIDE 44

"Jesus, I have been faithful to replace lies with Your truth. However, there seems to be an obstacle to my present progress. What do I need to focus upon or see?"

With gentle tenderness, Jesus looked affectionately and said, "My special treasure, we will continue to develop another strategic life lesson of learning to walk with Me in victory. That is to have an unoffendable spirit. That means you continually walk in forgiveness. I hope you won't pull away from Me. Forgiveness is one of the most misunderstood truths because the enemy doesn't want you to have the liberty that such a walk releases.

"Forgiveness doesn't mean the person who did wrong deserves your forgiveness. I want you to have the fruit of forgiveness. Forgiveness doesn't mean you are not angry at what happened. However, you choose to direct that anger at the enemy. Your forgiveness of another's wrongs paralyzes the enemy. He has no power to match a forgiving spirit. Forgiving another does not mean you put yourself in harm's way again. We will talk more about that later.

"Forgiveness means you refuse to be in bondage to another's evil or controlled by their offenses. Your forgiveness reverses the curse of sin and leaves the vengeance for wrongs in My hands. If it is comforting to you to hear how I hate evil and what I do to evil ones who refuse to repent, listen to My words in Isaiah 25:10 (NIV): *'The hand of the Lord will rest on this mountain; but Moab will be trampled in their land as straw is trampled down in the manure.'* Moab represents the enemy here. I do hate evil!"

"I choose to hate evil also, my Lord. I will choose to forgive, releasing You and Your resurrection power for myself and for You to work on my behalf with others. Thank You, Jesus!"

(Meditate upon these Scriptures asking the Holy Spirit to work in your heart. See Matthew 6:14-15; 18:21-35, Isaiah 25:10; 1 Peter 3:12; and 3 John 11. Write down your commitment to Jesus.)

My Garden Within

_____

_____

_____

As He spoke those last words, Ally's heart became brighter with color. She watched as lilies bloomed before her eyes in yellow, pink, and orange, and tulips lifted their faces in every color imaginable. Life was taking place in her. Truth was taking place in her. Love was in her and surrounding her. The fragrance from these blooms filled her garden and her senses—the very fragrance of Jesus Himself!

Jesus broke into her thoughts, saying, "Even surrounded by these blooms, Ally, beware, because you do have an enemy. He will always try to plant weed seeds, even when things seem to be going so beautifully, and even while you are sleeping."

Ally remembered waking in the morning and looking at her garden at home only to find new weeds.

"The enemy is after your testimony. He is after your flourishing garden life, and he is after these blossoms," He said as He raised His hands over the newly opened flowers. "He tried to ruin and destroy it with quick-growing weeds. He is trying to confuse and frustrate you, and he is committed to that. His goal is to try to thwart My purpose for your life. He himself is a weed."

He held His arms out to the sides, and immediately Ally saw the cross behind Him. His voice then resounded as He proclaimed, "We overcome the enemy by the blood of the Lamb, Myself, and by the word of our testimony. You overcome him, the devil, by God's own power. God's power is released through you when you pray. Just talk to Him in everything. We are living inside you, here in you."

She looked around and saw the beauty of the Lord everywhere.

"Your words, Ally, can be like weeds or like blooms. Your words can either suffocate the enemy of your soul or oxygenate the enemy of your soul—just by what you say." He reached out and touched her mouth. "By the words you speak, you bring life or death."

Oh Lord, may I always feel Your hand touching my lips and guarding my words, Ally thought.

"It's all a choice; even intimate friendship with Me is a choice, not an accident. You must spend time with the Gardener, for I bring the change. When you seek Me, you will find Me, and we will tend to this garden. We will pull up the weeds together, and you will truly live."

DEVOTIONAL GUIDE 45

"Jesus, I do hate the weeds in my life. However, working with You to eliminate them makes it so much easier. Thank You so much. I want to remove every weed the enemy has sown and close all doors that have been open to his devilish schemes. I feel there is blockage to Your living water flowing into my soul. Can You tell me what it is?"

"Yes, My precious one, I can. I knew we would have to deal with this soon. I am glad you noticed and asked because I love to tell you the truth and watch you become more and more free.

"When one has been deeply wounded, held ungodly beliefs, or practiced carnal behavior for a period of time, opportunities for demonic entry occur. Satan looks for every opportunity to torment and destroy those I love. Unhealed wounds, unmet needs, and fleshly patterns provide an opportunity to set up shop in the garden of one's soul. You need not be afraid of the demonic, My precious one. All evil entities had to bow at the cross and must once again bow when found out and confronted. I have given you that authority. Because of time and resignation, ignorance or inattention, evil grows and expands into a stronghold where it can make a home. While there, the demonic continues to tell lies that keep you from My love and the life I have planned for you."

It is good to have your mentor pray with you regarding release from any demonic activity. For a longer prayer to guide, you can carefully read Appendix A. You can remove the demonic blockage yourself by saying something like the following:

> In the name of Jesus Christ, the true Jesus, by the power of His shed blood and through the anointing and leadership of the Holy Spirit, I now *renounce and break and loose* myself from the demonic bondage brought into my life by (abuse, my choices, traumatic experience, etc.). Using the authority given to me by Jesus, you must go be the footstool of Jesus as Psalm 110:1 says. I ask you, angels of God, to enforce this command now on any foreign, alien, or demonic entity present and to force compliance. I thank You, Lord Jesus Christ for setting me free. I confess, Lord, that I have given away part of myself, part of my control to the kingdom of darkness. I choose today to submit my life to the lordship of Jesus Christ and ask You, Lord, to reclaim and take back the ground I have lost. Fill these areas with the Holy Spirit, thereby bringing restoration. Thank You, Jesus, for answering my prayer. Amen.

"Guard your heart, My precious one, continue in forgiveness and walk with Me and not in the habits of the past. I am with you. I will strengthen you and hold you in My righteous right hand. This is your part in not giving in to the enemy again and walking forward in maturity."

"Thank You so much, Jesus. You are so faithful to show the way, the life, and the truth. I love You. I want to love You with all my mind, with all my soul, and with all my heart."

(Prayerfully read Luke 19:10, Revelation 12:11, Psalm 110:1, and Ephesians 6:11-18. Make notes of what you understand.)

My Garden  Within

_____

_____

_____

They began walking and came to a part of her soul that looked pretty good. He sat down, and she sat next to Him.

"Say your garden is looking really good, and then something happens in your life. Maybe someone didn't validate you or said something as you perceived as mean to you, and these seeds of weeds began to take root, and they started squeezing the life out of all God has done."

Ally began to think of a situation in her life when someone had recently hurt her feelings.

"Here lies the problem," He explained, looking into her eyes. "Sometimes you tend to the problem more than you tend to the plantings of the Lord."

Ally nodded in agreement.

"To *tend* is to apply one's attention. Problems and circumstances try to steal your attention away from Me, away from love, and away from what I am doing in your garden."

Ally blew her breath up at her bangs, as she knew she had done that very thing—and quite often.

"You tend to talk more about the problems than the answers or truth. Others may try to plant weeds in you, and the world will try to steal your full attention. Don't let those weeds, those lies, or worldly things grow in your garden, because weeds spread quickly. Be watchful. Be attentive, because they will try to crowd out, take over, and steal the nutrients from the things I have planted in you."

He paused, looking very attentive to something He was hearing.

"My advice to your new weed-watching department," He said, pointing to her brain, "is to give new invaders high priority and stop them before they get out of hand." He was smiling, because He knew He was enough.

Inside of her, she knew also that this King was enough, and the new truths blossoming around and within her kept her heart focused on the One who planted them there.

Jesus then reached down and pulled a stone from the sole of His shoe. It was a gray, unattractive stone. "To add to the others," He said. "I chose an ugly stone to remind you that the weeds are unattractive. They won't attract others to Me if your life and your actions are surrounded by them."

Ally slowly took the stone from His hand, wrinkled her nose at it, and added it to her previously acquired stones. "I hope this is the only ugly one," she said and glanced up from her little black pouch.

"Remember this when you look at the weed stone: Love the flowers; hate the weeds. Love good and hate evil."

Ally closed her eyes and nodded in acknowledgment, and when she opened them she found herself lying under a cedar tree.

DEVOTIONAL GUIDE 46

"Jesus, I want to focus on the problem of my emotions. I love the good emotions. However, I have tried to change my bad feelings but have been unsuccessful. I know I am not to repress or deny my emotions. What do I do?"

"You are right, My special love. Feelings or emotions are very legitimate. We (Father, Holy Spirit, and I) not only created emotions but We are also emotional. You simply can't comprehend the extravagant dimensions of Our love for you except as We reveal the breadth, test its length, plumb the depths, and rise to the heights. Our compassion for you, Our delight to be with you, and Our goodness toward you has no end. Likewise, Our anger at how the enemy has defiled, wounded, and abused you has no end. We are committed to restore all he has stolen from you."

"Jesus, I open the door to my damaged, defiled emotions. I cry out to You and say, 'I can't. You never said I could. You can and always said You would. Now, lay an ax to the root of any evil emotion or weed in the garden of my heart. Release the emotions of Your heart through me. I will cooperate in any way You reveal to me. I want to fulfill the destiny You saw before the foundation of the world.'"

Jesus smiled with delight. "It is done, My precious love!"

Jesus continued saying, "My precious love, remember feelings are, with a few exceptions, good servants but they are disastrous masters. Walk with an open heart to Me allowing Me to enable you to sort out the precious feelings from the vile feelings. Do not get involved in seeking to change the bad feelings by way of a head-on resistance or a redirection of them by your 'willpower' confrontation. That does not work.

"Thoughts generate feelings. Your brain and mind are uniquely connected. Your brain and mind direct your emotions. What you are thinking is what you will become. Restore and rebuild your emotions by thinking about who I am, what I have done for you, and how much I love you. Focus on My faithfulness to you, My goodness poured out for you, and My great power to accomplish all that needs to be done for your wholeness. Thank Me for all you see around you that reflects My glory."

"Jesus, I love You so much. Thank You for redirecting me emotionally. You are the best treasure ever! Through Your resurrection power my emotions will be healed."

(Soak in the following Scriptures: Matthew 3:10; Ephesians 3:14-21; John 19:30; and Isaiah 26:3. Carefully record your inspiration.)

My Garden Within

Devotional Guide Inventory Chapter 10

1. What causes trauma and wounds? What has Jesus done so that pain may be healed? What part of your soul usually holds the pain? Why does healing often take an extended amount of time? How do you gain authority for your freedom and others? What is a key element in processing healing? How are you to nurture your emotions in the healing process? What must your emotions do to receive healing?

2. Why is a mentor advisable in processing your healing time? What does Scripture say about your needs for others' counsel? How can you find a mature mentor or one who is a few steps ahead of you in bringing your emotions to wholeness? What are two wrong ways of thinking about you? Which one do you need to work on?

3. How do you "put off" the shame, guilt, and unworthiness and "put on" the truth? Where do you send the lies? How can you remind yourself to actively practice your part of filling the ditch made in your soul with truth? What is your plan for removing the lies and establishing truth?

4. What does forgiveness do for the person who forgives? Why is it critical for you to forgive? How are you to direct your anger toward the evil done to you and others? How does Jesus feel about evil?

5. What is a blockage to your healing besides lack of forgiveness? How is this handled? Has Jesus given you authority over demonic influence? How could a mature mentor be helpful in

such prayer times? After the eviction of evil entities, what is your job regarding your heart?

6. Are feelings to control your life? What is the wrong way to handle bad emotions? After you release your negative feelings to Jesus, what are you to focus on to positively affect your emotions?

My Garden Within Inventory

_____

_____

_____

_____

_____

_____

_____

_____

_____

_____

_____

_____

_____

_____

_____

_____

_____

_____

_____

_____

CHAPTER 11

Under the Cedar Tree

May Christ, through your faith, [actually] dwell (settle down, abide, make His permanent home) in your hearts! May you be rooted deep in love and founded securely on love, that you may have the power and be strong to apprehend and grasp with all the saints [God's devoted people, the experience of that love] what is the breadth and length and height and depth [of it]; [that you may really come] to know [practically, through experience for yourselves] the love of Christ, which far surpasses mere knowledge [without experience]; that you may be filled [through all your being] unto all the fullness of God...and become a body wholly filled and flooded with God Himself! (Ephesians 3:17-19)

Ally lay on the ground in some lavish, green grass, looking up through the cedar's hearty branches. She looked to her side, and Jesus was lying beside her.

"Did you know that cedar is the strongest or hardiest type of wood there is?" He asked.

Ally shook her head and replied, "No, I did not."

"It is because of the tenacity of its roots. I want you to be rooted and grounded in Me, and I will make you strong like this cedar here."

Ally watched as the massive tree branches moved so elegantly in the gentle breeze that started blowing around them.

"I am going to teach you now about your thoughts, Ally. You need to train them to be rooted and founded in Me and Me alone, and I will make you strong and immovable. You need to learn to take every single thought that comes into your mind into captivity. What I mean by that is this: You do not need to let every thought that comes into your mind have full freedom in you. You do have a bit of control over your thoughts, if you do not let them take you everywhere they want to. You need to grab hold of them when they come in and restrain them. Don't let them just run freely through your mind, but grasp them firmly, and bring every one of them to Me."

Ally thought about how many thoughts had taken up residence in her mind and were roaming about, free and unrestrained.

"You need to deprive these thoughts of freedom and liberty and ask yourself these questions: 'Is this truth? Is this thought from God? Or does it come from the enemy of my soul? Does this thought bring life or death?' If death, then withstand these thoughts initially, when they first enter. Bring them to Me. Be rooted in Me and these truths I am teaching you and you will be established, strong, and immovable, just like this cedar tree."

DEVOTIONAL GUIDE 47

"Jesus, I do want to lead every thought captive to You. I have the thought often that says, 'It's someone else's fault I am angry, irritated, or upset. If they were out of my life or if they would act differently toward me, everything would be all right.' Help me to process a thought like this."

"My beloved, you are wrestling with a universal problem that plagues the majority of My people. To blame someone else is a refusal to take responsibility for your own actions or behavior. We have been bringing healing to the areas in which you were truly victimized; where shame, guilt and condemnation were placed upon you through no fault of your own. However, *now* from this point onward it is right to lead such wrong thoughts to Me and begin taking responsibility for them. As a matter of fact, I want you to ask yourself this question, 'What in me would cause me to feel_____?' For instance, what is in me that would cause such anger, fear, or irritation?

"My words written down in Mark say, '*There is nothing that enters a man from outside which can defile him; but the things which come out of him, those are the things that defile a man. ...For from within, out of the heart of men, proceed evil thoughts...*' (Mark 7:15, 21 NKJV). All these evil things come from within and defile a person.

"My beloved, when you think your anger, fear, and irritations are caused by someone else, immediately run to Me. If necessary, stay in your quiet place until the emotion settles down enough for you to proceed healthfully onward with Me. Give Me your negative emotion and ask Me to help you to know at what you are really angry, fearful, or irritated. Invite Me to begin dissolving, unhooking, and releasing you from the enemy's hook within that has blamed another rather than solving it appropriately. Ask Me to show you where the enemy got a hook into you resulting in the anger, fear, or irritation you are now manifesting. It could have been a big or smaller incident where the enemy told you a lie or violated you thereby creating this mountain of destructive emotions. As I expose it and you release it to Me, the root is chopped out. Healing is then released."

"Yes, Jesus, I will cooperate with You. When I feel like blaming another, defending myself, I will turn to You to unpack your provision for my destructive emotions that have not been dealt with. Thank You for helping me become a responsible, whole person so we can get to the root of the problem and walk in victory."

(Carefully and prayerfully read Mark 7:15, 20-23 and Romans 8:37. Make note of your conclusions and your resolve to face such problems in the future.)

My Garden Within

_____

_____

_____

Ally looked again at the majestic tree and then found herself back in the vineyard with Jesus. It had perfect rows of grapevines growing inside her.

They came upon a wild vine branch that had grown away from the main vine. She knew that the main vine was a symbol of Jesus Himself because of the Scripture that talked about Him being the true vine.

Jesus continued talking as He took this wild vine, brought it back, and attached it to the main vine. As He did this He said, "Don't think and set your feelings on the thoughts the enemy puts in your mind and let them have free rein in you. But bring them back and attach them to the sturdy, stable, fixed, sure vine—the truth. Me. Attach every thought to Me. And we will cut off and remove all that is not truth, but lies. Set your mind and keep it set on what is above, the higher things, and not on the things that are of the earth."

"What do you mean by set my mind?" Ally asked, trying to apply this truth.

Jesus then fastened the wild vine firmly with a strap that He retrieved from His pocket. "Set means to put in a specific position or state or to put in a stable position. It means to fix...so fix your thoughts on Me, Ally." He smiled with His eyes. "It means to restore to a proper and normal state when dislocated or broken, like setting a bone when an arm is broken."

"Some of my thinking is broken, I'm sure."

"Yes, sometimes your mind or thoughts are a little dislocated. They are thrown into confusion or disorder when they are disrupted by lies. You know, Ally, the enemy of your soul wants to disrupt the flow and the plan of God for you. He wants to throw you into confusion, put you out of proper relationship, and displace you. He wants to put you in a place of doubt."

Ally thought about how frequently doubt and insecurity took up residence in her thoughts.

"Bring every thought before Me, and I will adjust those thoughts for proper functioning. I will put you in a stable position that is resistant to sudden changes and to the negative thoughts that the enemy plants.

When negative thoughts first come, at the beginning of an attack on your mind, be firm and immoveable. Right then set your thoughts on Me, on My truth. Fasten those thoughts to Me."

DEVOTIONAL GUIDE 48

"Jesus, I am feeling that one of the wildest, strongest vines in my inner garden that has grown away from the main vine, is self-pity. I have heard this called staring at my 'belly button' syndrome which is looking at me instead of God. I want my entire inner vines to be pliable in Your hands. Help me to unravel the truths of self-pity."

Jesus was ecstatic about unraveling this diabolical, insidious lie from the enemy. He knew I was really serious about growing in Him and this was part of my answer. Jesus said with empathy in His voice, "My beloved, I hate what the enemy has done to My family. When sin entered the human race, self-centeredness replaced God-consciousness. When self replaces Me, My life is blocked because you are trying to meet your needs your way. Self-pity is among the worse of sins.

"To indulge in self-pity is to say I have not done well for you, My provision is not enough, and Father's plan is not perfect. You hinder yourself from receiving My grace and you block others from entering into My provision when you nurse self-pity in yourself or others.

"Why did I forcefully refuse Peter's sympathy when he tried to spare Me the suffering of the cross? I knew I could receive sympathy from My Father only, and from the angels in heaven. So I said to Peter, "Get behind Me, Satan! You are an offense to Me, for you are not mindful of the things of God, but the things of men." You, My beloved, must do the same!

"Learn from Me, My beloved. Let Me lead as I let My Father lead. Let Me be in the driver's seat. Don't run from suffering; embrace it as I did. Self-sacrifice is the way to finding yourself, your true self. When you die to your way of meeting your needs and surrender to My way, you not only gain the true life of your soul but you also release My Kingdom to earth for others to receive."

"Thank You, Jesus. I refuse to surrender my strength and vitality to the enemy by feeding in myself or another's sin of self-pity. I will not throw a 'pity party' for myself or attend another's 'pity party.' This dislocated or broken part of my inner garden is released to You to be restored. What a joy to grow with You, Jesus!"

(Ponder the following Scriptures asking the Holy Spirit to open your eyes to His present truth for you: Matthew 16:21-28 and Luke 15:10. Record your thoughts.)

My Garden Within

_____

_____

_____

He came upon another vine that was running wild in her vineyard. "You see, these thoughts seek to devour you and this garden life. They seek your time and your devotion. The enemy wants to take up residence in your thought life. He wants his lies to live in you, and he is very subtle, so he sneaks in. Guard your garden, and guard your thoughts."

She took in a deep breath as Jesus continued.

"Ally, let Me tell you a story. I once went by the field of a lazy man and by the vineyard of a man devoid of understanding. I was in another garden, and behold, it was all grown over with thorns. Nettles were covering its face, and its stone wall was broken down. Then this man beheld Me and considered what he was letting control his life. He received instruction, and his garden came back to life. Don't be lazy about taking your thoughts captive, or they could take over your garden."

Again, Ally considered how she had let her garden get so weed-filled and overcrowded with wrong thoughts.

"Spend time with Me, Ally; get understanding, and you will truly live. It takes a little work to take every thought into captivity, but be strong and encourage yourself in Me. Ask for My thoughts and My perspective, and I will give them to you."

They walked up to a dry, withered shrub.

"If the lazy man had not turned his mind, thoughts, and heart to Me, he would have remained like a shrub destitute in the desert. He would not have seen any good come, but he would have dwelled in the parched, dry places in the wilderness and in uninhabited, salty land."

The shrub then totally transformed before their eyes into a strong tree with lots of fruit hanging from its branches.

"But instead, he believed in Me and trusted in Me. He made Me his hope and his confidence. And now, because he has stopped letting his thoughts run free in him and relies on Me, he shall be like a tree planted by the waters that spreads out its roots by the river. He, like you now, Ally, will not see and fear when heat comes; his and your leaves shall be green. You will not be anxious and full of care, and you will not cease yielding fruit. The people of this world need Me, Ally; they are dying. I want to feed them as I am feeding you. Will you hold out to the world this truth, this life? Will you live your life to give Me out to them? I am the fruit in you. I am the way and the truth, and I am this life."

As He said this, He pulled off a piece of fruit from the tree before them.

"They need Me. They may not know it yet, but they will. I put in all humankind this void that only I can fill. Can I use you? To hold out life?"

He handed Ally the fruit; they began walking, and He continued to talk about thoughts.

"If you sow good thoughts in the soil of your mind, the fruit that comes from it will be life-giving and nourishing to yourself and to others."

DEVOTIONAL GUIDE 49

"Jesus, I want to be completely devoted to You, leading my thoughts captive to You. Never do I want to be like the lazy man about whom you spoke. I want to dwell in my promise land rather than having my land be a parched, dry, salty, and uninhabited wilderness. How can I know if I have led my thoughts successfully to You or if my thoughts are sinful?"

Jesus was glad to address the confusion the enemy often brings. With a sparkle in His eyes, He said, "My beloved, every wrong thought that comes into your mind is not sin. It is what you do with that thought that determines whether or not it becomes sin. Have you heard the old saying, 'You cannot keep a bird from flying over, but you can keep it from building in a nest on your head?' This is much the same. When a thought walks across your mind, you can either invite it to sit down and become part of you or you can say return to sender. If you embrace the carnal, fleshly thought, your lustful flesh will get pregnant, and have a baby—sin! Sin then grows up to adulthood, and becomes a real killer.

"As you walk in companionship with Me, Holy Spirit will enable you to recognize whether your thoughts are precious or vile. If vile and as a result of bad habits, you will engage in old practices. You need to apply My shed blood to your lustful, lazy thoughts. Turn from the habit to Me and continue our sweet fellowship. The Holy Spirit will show you through conviction or He may use someone else to point out you are not acting like yourself in Me and have reverted to the old carnal you. Simply be ready to hear, ready to obey, and I will take care of the rest! There is no need for you to become overly concerned with being perfect. Do your best, and I will cover the rest as you continue trusting in Me."

"The good news really is good news, Jesus. Thank You for helping me sow good thoughts so that our harvest within me and for others will be great! I love walking with You!"

(Study James 1:12-18 and Galatians 6:6-10. Write down helpful points for your journey.)

My Garden Within

_____

_____

_____

She looked at the fruit in the palm of her hand. *Life,* she thought.

"Think about *what* you are thinking, Ally, because your life will move in the direction of your strongest thoughts. If you don't manage your thought life"—He paused to catch her gaze—"you won't manage your life. Don't continue to allow negative thoughts to manage your life anymore. Choose, Ally, to close your thoughts to the things you cannot change, and move forward. There are too many good things in life to allow things beyond your control to destroy you and your garden life. Don't choose to follow bad thoughts any further, because they will lead you down a path of destruction."

Jesus turned, and they began to move in a different direction. "Rather, decide to change direction again and again and again. Choose life and good thoughts until that becomes your habit."

Ally continued to follow Him; in every footstep she was witnessing His life continuing to form in her.

"Do you know what repentance is? It is when you decide to choose life and you turn your life and move in a different direction. It is to think differently from what you used to think. Change your life, turn to Me, and walk in this new direction with Me, like you just did, and new fruit will come."

Ally again looked at the piece of fruit in her hand.

"You can feed this fruit to others and help them to live again."

They found themselves again under the cedar tree. Ally thought about Jesus first telling her that the cedar was the strongest tree because of its strong root system.

Jesus then asked, "Ally, do you see the roots?"

Ally shook her head. "No," she replied.

"That is because they are underground, unseen by others. Roots are the part of the tree or plant that serves as its support. Roots draw food for the plant and water from surrounding soil, and they also store food. It's the secret place, unseen by others, where it is just you and Me. Just like these roots, the secret place and that time with just the two of us is the base, support, or root source of the life I am creating in you. It is an essential part of this garden life and is needed for growth."

Ally adored this new garden life and this new relationship with her Beloved. She loved the life she now felt inside her. She actually felt beautiful. She said, "I want the roots of my being and who I am to be firmly and deeply planted in You. Never before have I felt this beautiful or this alive, and it's You, Lord. It's all You."

Tears began to fall onto her cheeks as she looked into His big, brown eyes. "Keep me so rooted in You that the enemy cannot get to those deep inner thoughts of my heart anymore. I want to remain wrapped up in You, for I belong to You."

DEVOTIONAL GUIDE 50

"Jesus, I want You to be my root system and for all my roots to be firmly established in You and only You. I am realizing You are the only source of true life. The beauty and love I am beginning to experience is Your life in me. Is there a deeper level of establishing my roots in You that I have not embraced?"

Jesus looked intently and said, "Yes, My beloved. This deeper establishment of your roots in Me addresses how you are joined to those closest to you. Listen to My words written down in Luke 14:26, *'If anyone comes to Me and does not hate his [own] father and mother [in the sense of indifference to or relative disregard for them in comparison with his attitude toward God] and [likewise] his wife and children and brothers and sisters—[yes] and even his own life also—he cannot be My disciple.'* Note the word hate doesn't literally mean you hate your loved ones, but it is a comparison emphasizing the degree of devotion to Me as opposed to your loved ones. I must be first.

"My beloved, take a deep breath and know My heart. I am establishing your belongingness to Me in order that you truly become free to full capacity with My life so that My life in you will flow out to others. As you began growing in Me, I used others to lead you to Me. It is hard, however, at times to not seek life from the ones you love and who helped you rather than Me. They were there for a season to bring you to Me, but now you must turn loose of their hands to fully hold My hand. This can be scary. However, it will establish your root system in Me.

"Also, if you have been inordinately attached to another in a wrong way, those inordinate soul ties must be broken. Many times we end up in a relationship in which we are getting our needs met through another or they are getting needs met through us in a way that is unhealthy. It may be a special relationship, but it needs to be corrected so I am the provision of life and not one another."

Appendix B gives you a sample prayer to pray as He shows you any codependent, inordinate soul ties that need to be severed. After you break soul ties through prayer, you will learn to walk in full dependency upon Him experiencing freedom for you and giving the other person the same chance to know and taste Him.

"Jesus, I am depending upon You to strengthen and uphold me in this time of cleaving only to You, thereby establishing my roots deeply in You. Thank You for loving me enough to show me the truth."

(Prayerfully read the following Scriptures: Luke 14:26 and Hebrews 4:12. Ponder and write down your insights.)

My Garden Within

Jesus smiled, because her last statement tied into the next meaning of what it meant to be rooted in Him that He wanted to share with her.

"Being rooted is being settled into, or belonging to. You do belong to Me. I bought you with My precious blood, and you and so many others belong to the family of God. Many times you asked, 'Where do I belong, God?' Well, you belong with Me, with Us."

Ally smiled and thought about the significance of the word *belong*.

"It also means to be fully settled or entrenched. The secret place in Me, Ally, is like a trench, and a trench is especially used for the purpose of fortifying and defending. It is a place of security. You are secure in Me.

In this place I will strengthen you. I will add more and more strength, and I will provide moral and mental strength by adding extra support—just like the roots of this tree."

He placed His hand on her heart. "Here in the secret place I will give life to you, and I will fill you with strength and courage. I will inspire you here, and I will guide you by divine influence. I will fill you with noble and reverent emotion, and I will stimulate you to creativity and action. I will breathe life into you here so that you can then impart this life." He held up Ally's hand, which still had the piece of fruit in it, and said, "Feed My sheep, Ally. Bring them into My presence and into this way of life. I don't want any to perish…I want all to come to this place of life and security."

Ally closed her eyes and held the piece of fruit with both hands, and again she saw a sea of faces before her. She began to encourage them with these words.

"When circumstances and situations surround you that seem dark and dreary, jump into God's trench. It's like an army's trench but safer. You are so safe there. Jump into the garden, the secret place, His trench, and let Him fortify you there. When the enemy is shooting his fiery darts at you, jump into the trench! Jump into the secret place and let God invigorate you. Let Him impart His strength and courage to you! Let Him breathe His life into you and give you life. Let Him fill you with His Spirit and inspire you to be active on His behalf! Let Him guide and arouse you by His divine influence! Let Him fill you with reverent emotion and stimulate you to creativity and action! Let Him defend you, for He is your defender. Let Him protect you and keep you. Let Him live in you and for you!"

She could actually feel His life flowing from her being, just like He said when He told her about His rivers flowing from her. "Being rooted in Him like this is necessary for growth. Stay attached to the sure vine and to the truth. You cannot truly live without being rooted deeply in Him and in His love." She ended her encouraging words with this firm statement: "You are loved."

Ally was amazed by the crowd of hearts that stood before her. She could actually see them being transformed before her. She saw some weeping, some laughing, and some praying, but all of them were grasping the truth she was revealing to them. When this vision ended, she opened her eyes and saw that the fruit in her hand had turned into her eighth stone. Yellow in color, and it looked like it had roots running through it. She slipped her little black pouch out of her pocket and added to it this new precious stone.

Rooted in Him, she thought. She looked around her heart, her garden. She couldn't see Jesus any longer, but she knew that He was still with her, and the fruit tree remained.

Strong.

Immovable.

DEVOTIONAL GUIDE 51

"I am Yours, Jesus, and You are mine! What peace such a truth resonates in my heart. As I run to You, Jesus, into God's trench, is that like dwelling in the secret place of the Most High where I am stable? Also, is that where my soul is synchronized and flows with my human spirit?"

Jesus responded with exuberance saying, "My beloved, not only are you really getting what I have to say to you, but you are also asking some deep questions that thrill My heart to answer.

"Yes, being rooted in Me, being safe and secure in My trench is exactly like I wrote about in Psalm 91. It is in this place of trusting Me to be your fortress and refuge that no foe can withstand. You are safe in Me.

"Because you have done the hard soul work in your garden within, are you ready to trust Me with synchronizing, and bringing into unity, and aligning the parts of your soul that have worked separately to allow you to survive? You were injured because your choice was violated. I will not do that. Your soul is made up of three components: mind, will, and emotions. In other words, a person's soul has thoughts, makes choices, and has feelings. May I have permission to address your soul by speaking to these areas?"

"Yes, Jesus, You are my life and I trust You."

"Thank you, My beloved. I speak first to your human spirit and say you have done a marvelous job of keeping your eyes upon Me and receiving your measure of grace that I have allotted for you each day. You have allowed Me to bless you and you have received My blessings. Now, I want to speak directly to the three areas of your soul.

"Soul, I applaud you for having survived so well considering the inability of Will, Mind, and Emotion to work as a team. Now is the time to unite Will, Mind, and Emotion and move from surviving to thriving. Every person was created with a soul containing three precious parts: will, mind, and emotions in which each has a special assignment. However, apart from Me you aren't able to process intense trauma. Trauma causes deep pain and confusion in which each part can separate into a role of survival. Survival is good, but you were created for a unity centered on Me. You can only be all I've created you to be when you are unified and flowing together as one. To minister to every special part of you, let's speak to each as an individual. Let's start with your will, which is your choice.

"Will, you have done an admirable job in holding the soul together. You have protected Mind from experiencing all the painful emotions it could not handle and still function. Because Emotion has opened the door for healing, Emotion doesn't need to be separate from Will and Mind anymore. The healing process is in motion. Mind can now embrace emotions incorporating the mind of Christ, bringing wholeness to everyone.

"Will, you can now trust Jesus in God's trench where problems are resolved to coordinate a healthy companionship between you, Mind, and Emotion. Each will honor the other and consider each other's perspective. Will, you are to allow Emotion and Mind to interact until there is peace between them. Will, lay aside the need to protect knowing I am here to bring about reconciliation. When Will, Mind, and Emotion are in agreement being the team I designed them to be, they together submit to the leadership of your human spirit led by the Holy Spirit.

"I declare the synchronization and unity begin flowing. Soul, you have worked so hard. It is time now you rest and do only what you were designed to do. Snuggle up under the human spirit, who is directly connected with God, and enjoy being a bridge as you interpret what the human spirit receives from God. As My Spirit flows through your human spirit and into your soul, wholeness is being birthed.

"This is thriving, My beloved! Let's settle down for a lifetime of learning to thrive together as we process life's journey. Maturity happens this way."

"Thank You, Jesus, for allowing me to be completely rooted in You so my garden will grow, producing fruit that remains."

(Prayerfully meditate upon the following Scriptures: Psalms 91:1-4; 51:6; 86:11-12; Philippians 2:13; Song of Solomon 2:14; and 1 Thessalonians 5:23. Write down what Jesus is impressing upon your heart.)

My Garden Within

_____

_____

_____

Devotional Guide Inventory Chapter 11

1. Can another person *make you* angry, irritable, or ignite fear in you? From where does the negative emotion come? Does another cause the problem or simply expose your inner problem? Why must you assume responsibility for negative emotions? What is the productive way to deal with negative emotions?

2. What is a prime fleshly example of how sin affects your focus? Why is self-pity so evil? What can you learn from how Jesus dealt with Peter when he expressed self-pity toward Him? What is one major key to finding your true self?

3. Does having a wrong thought mean that you have sinned? How does a wrong thought become sin? How do you know if a thought is vile or precious? What safety net has Jesus provided for successfully leading your thoughts to Him? What is your part?

4. Are family and loved ones gifts from God? When do they become an obstacle rather than an asset? Who must have preeminence in your life? What needs to be done in order to sever the unhealthy parts of a codependent, inordinate relationship? Once the spiritual hold is released, will you have to establish a new relationship through godly boundaries?

5. What does God's trench or the secret dwelling place in Psalm 91 describe? Why is this needed? What happens to your soul when trauma and painful circumstances are not processed in Jesus' presence? What is the difference between surviving and thriving? How are the parts of the soul—will, mind, and

emotions—unified? Will this be an ongoing process to keep the soul unified? When the soul is thriving, what is its primary responsibility? How should the human spirit, soul, and body function in relationship to each other?

My Garden Within Inventory

_____

_____

_____

_____

_____

_____

_____

_____

_____

_____

_____

_____

_____

_____

_____

_____

_____

_____

_____

_____

_____

CHAPTER 12

You Look Just Like Your Heavenly Father

...Behold, as the clay is in the potter's hand, so are you in My hand... (Jeremiah 18:6).

The next afternoon, in the soft breezes of a lovely summer day, Ally tended the garden at her house. She came upon a dahlia that had been crushed and lay lifeless at her feet. She was perplexed by the devastation of this once tall, upright, beautiful flower.

At once she found herself before a door, which had an antique, rounded top that appeared to have been made from different pieces of rosewood crafted together. In the middle of the door, on a golden plate, was the inscription "Potter's House" and below that an invitation to "Come In."

As she pushed open the heavy door, she saw Him, the One whom her soul loved. He was working at the potter's wheel, spinning a beautiful pot. She watched Him as He so lovingly and delicately shaped the vessel with His hands. He pulled up on the sides so as to make it taller and smoother. He dipped His hands in a bucket to get more water and returned to His masterpiece.

Suddenly the piece He was making began to wobble and fall apart in His hands, so He made it over, reworking it into another vessel as it seemed good for Him to make. He then lifted His beautiful, shining eyes to meet Ally's focused, unbroken gaze.

"Can I do with you, Ally, as I have done with this vessel? Can I remake you? For as this clay is in My hands, so are you in My hands."

"Um…" she paused for a second, "but You just crushed that vessel into a lump of clay. Will it hurt, Lord?"

"It will only hurt your ways of doing and being. For I know what I have planned for you, Ally. Can you trust Me? Will you just crawl into My hands and let Me mold you into the vessel that will escort you into your destiny?"

Ally's face fell, as she was a little apprehensive to answer His question.

"I have known what I have been making you, Ally, through all you have been through already. Sometimes you have wanted to look like others or be like others and have strived with Me. You have said to the One fashioning you, 'What do You think You are making?' or 'Where are my handles?'"

Ally immediately thought of a time when she desired to be like someone else and had compared herself to this person.

"I never intended My vessels to compete with each other; I want you to complete each other—to celebrate and encourage each other's strengths while finding out who I created you to be."

☙DEVOTIONAL GUIDE 52❧

"Jesus, You are the One whom my soul loves. I am gradually learning to trust You. The Potter's House sounds scary because I am afraid of pain. Coupled with the idea of looking like my heavenly Father, I am thrown into a panic, as I sometimes envision only my earthly father, which for me isn't a good thing. So the thought of my heavenly Father scares me. What do I do, Jesus?"

Jesus understood as only He can. He understands the traumas within. With a tender, compassionate smile, He said, "Thank you for being honest about what you feel, My precious love. The enemy is a master at seeking to keep you from life, Our life. So many human authorities misrepresent Father's heart. This fact breaks His heart and Mine. When that happens, the plan of the enemy is released to keep Father's children from trusting Him, seeing His heart and receiving His love. In other words, from being fully alive! Living life to the fullest abundantly.

"Remember when we talked about the necessity of separating the precious from the vile? When authorities misrepresent My love, know they are blind, deceived, and being used by the enemy. Release them into My care and seek My response to them. We will talk more about this soon.

"For now, know the trust you have for Me is the same as having trust in Father. Why? Because the one who loves and trusts Me, loves and trusts Father. While I was on earth, Philip asked Me to show My disciples the Father. My words to him are My words to you also, 'He who has seen Me has seen the Father....' My precious one, it will take some time, but begin meditating upon this truth. As I say in My Word, you love Me, trust Me, and are walking with Me because Father *drew* you to Me. His plan has always been to love you. His heart beats for you. His heart longs for His children to come home back into His heart. The enemy knows this truth and seeks to rob you from Our love. Father and I are One. Bask in the truth."

"Thank You, Jesus, for fashioning me into the beautiful 'pot' You know I will enjoy being. I am choosing not to seek to look like others but rather look like You and my heavenly Father. Open my eyes, Holy Spirit, to see the truth as I soak in Jesus' words."

(Prayerfully read with an open heart Jesus' words in John 10:25-30; 6:44-46; 14:7-11; 16:26-27; and 17:21. Write down the revelation you are receiving. Review it daily until it is part of you.)

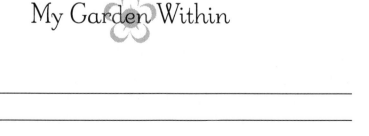

My Garden Within

_____

_____

_____

Ally looked up at some shelving that was filled with a lot of different vessels. Some were tall and slender, some were shorter and wider, and some were painted and shiny. Still other vessels had just recently been shaped by the Master's hand and were waiting to go into the fire so that they would retain their shape forever.

Jesus walked over to a big basin and began washing His hands. He looked back at Ally with a sneaky grin on His face and then turned and splattered her with the water left on His hands. It took her by surprise that He could be so serious yet so much fun all at the same time. She giggled as she wiped her face with her hand, keeping her gaze locked on Him.

He then nodded His head at her, indicating she should follow Him into the next room.

They entered, and her breath was taken away. Before them was the most brilliant table she had ever seen. It had every kind of flower, tree, and plant she had ever laid eyes on, plus ones she'd never seen carved into the surface of the table. Not a flaw was on this table, for it was perfectly formed by a Master Craftsman.

"This is My Father's table," Jesus said, "and I made it for Him. It is a place of revelation, and it is a place of introducing realities—a place where you receive your true identity."

He pulled out a chair. "Sit," He invited.

Ally's eyes grew huge as she looked at Him, and she slowly sat in the chair He had pulled out for her. Then He gently pushed her up to the table.

In her heart, she heard, *"Find your identity in Him."*

On the table before her was a small golden vial with the word *spikenard* written across it in silver pewter.

With tears welling up in His eyes, Jesus said, "This spikenard is a costly fragrance, and the plant must be crushed in order to make this perfume. Only then is the oil extracted. It represents worship. God, the Father, loves Me and wants to give Me a beautiful bride who loves Me extravagantly. You are at His table right now, sitting with Me, your Groom to be."

Ally closed her eyes and saw the picture of the cross with Jesus crushed, bruised, and bleeding before her. She grabbed the small vial before her and drank the perfume. She really didn't understand why, but she knew that she wanted worship to be in her. She wanted this costly perfume that He'd paid for with the stripes He took for her at the cross to come alive inside of her vessel.

"Your identity is who you are to Me. Ally, come to this table often and revelation will come. Revelation is the clear and often sudden ability to really understand the things I have to say to you, or that I want you to learn. These things are covered right now but will be revealed as you come. This table of revelation is for unearthing something that has been covered. It will be a place of greater insight and discovery for you. I will make Myself known here. I will fill you with light here and cause you to shine; then you can in turn give out that light. It is a place of spiritual understanding or insight of Me."

DEVOTIONAL GUIDE 53

"Jesus, when I look upon You on the cross giving Your all for me, I want to give my all for You. Please give me revelation on how trusting You while forgiving others, but not putting myself in harm's way, works. I want to find my identity in You, not others or my abuse."

Jesus was so thrilled to address these pivotal issues. With delight in His eyes and much tenderness, He said, "My precious love, thanks for asking. It is critical that your total identity be in Me. The enemy does everything he can to rob, steal, and destroy your true identity.

"When you forgive others for, let's say, misrepresenting Father's love, that is an act between you and Me. No one else needs to know or be involved. It is a one-way street. By forgiving, you open your heart to Me and remove the obstacle the enemy desired to use to block My power and love from coming to you. However, because you have forgiven people does not mean you are to trust them. You may or may not be reconciled with them. More will be said about this later. Trust grows and needs to be verified that there has really been a change in them.

To trust them when there hasn't been such a change is not only wrong for you, but does not truly love the others. It is being an accomplice to their carnal fleshly crime. Let's say you are driving the getaway car for a robbery. You didn't rob the bank, but you aided and abetted the criminals' getaway. You were part of the crime. Likewise, you are not to encourage or contribute to their carnal, fleshly activities through approval or support.

"If you allow further abuse, validate, or agree with fleshy living, you are hurting both yourself and them. I am living inside you and have given you the charge to make good choices for your well-being. When you do not support or agree with others' carnal actions, you are showing them love—real love. You are allowing them to taste the consequences that come from evil actions. The consequences are designed as a wake-up call to turn to Me for true life. In other words, the consequences are meant to bring repentance, which is turning from their way to My way of living. Often you must stand in My presence for a season allowing their misery factor to become stronger than their resistance to the truth. Your lack of support and friendship can be used by Me to cause them to suffer the loss their ungodly behavior produces. Hopefully they will become miserable enough to want to receive the truth and allow Me to change them.

"Yes, I know this is really hard, especially if your identity has come from receiving their approval. When you drink the spikenard, which means you are totally surrendered to Me, you allow all that is not of Me to be crushed. You are then giving of yourself to Me as I gave myself to you. It is worth it, My precious love. This is called becoming fully alive in Me."

"I willingly drink of the costly fragrance, spikenard, because I truly want to love You with all my heart, with all my mind, and with all my soul. Have Your way, Jesus!"

(Meditate upon the following Scriptures: Mark 12:30-31 and Galatians 6:7-9. Write down what you understand along with your commitment to trust Him in new ways.)

My Garden Within

_____

_____

_____

Ally looked into the polished surface of the table and saw her reflection shining back at her.

"Here is the first revelation."

Once again His words captured her attention.

"You are made in Our image. At My table this truth will become a reality to you so that when you go out into your community they will say of you, 'You look just like your Father.' That is what happens here; you begin to take on Our characteristics and Our behaviors because you have been here. You know you become like those you spend time with. You will look like Me to the world when you spend time with Me. I will fashion you as I have these pots," He said, looking up at the finished vessels that also filled the shelves in this room, "to look just like Me."

Ally felt excitement flow through her whole body.

"May I tell you a little about what it means to be made in Our image, the image of the Father, the Son, and the Holy Spirit?"

Ally loved being at this table of revelation, for it felt as if life itself, His life, was filling her. "Yes," she replied.

"An image is the reproduction of the form of someone," He said and then grabbed a vessel of gold from a shelf. "For example, a sculptured likeness." He took His sleeve and rubbed a little smudge off the surface of it. "When I say reproduction, I mean that it is something re-produced, or made again, from the original."

He put His hand on His chest, lifted His head high, and said, "I am the original." He looked back down at her and grinned. "It also means something duplicated, which means it's identically copied from an original or from a close or exact resemblance of another. So *resemblance* means similar in nature, form, and appearance, and to have a likeness to. It is as if someone were to say, 'You act just like your heavenly Father.'"

He set the vessel on the table. "Another meaning of reproduce is *imitate,* like an imitative appearance. You know, like Elvis?"

That reference caught Ally off guard. Of course—why wouldn't He know about Elvis and his impersonators? She laughed as Jesus stood up and did His best Elvis impersonation, dancing around her.

"They come in and look like him, act like him, move like him, and sing like him." He stopped dancing. "I want you to imitate Me." He sat back down with her at the table. "Here is the meaning of *imitate.*"

Ally was smiling; she greatly loved this table of Him, revealing truth to her.

"*Imitate* means to model oneself after the behavior or actions of another or to copy or mimic someone's actions, appearance, mannerisms, or speech. It means to copy exactly, to resemble, or to picture mentally and imagine. Picture yourself like Me, for you are, Ally, made in My image. When you spend time with Me in the garden and at this table, you will begin to look like Me, act like Me, and talk like Me." He smiled at her.

She smiled back as she began to imitate Him. He rested His chin upon His hand, and she did the same. He then made prayer hands and lifted them to His nose, and she did the same. He scratched His head and Ally mimicked that. Jesus then threw back His head and gave a big belly laugh.

"You are so silly," He said, and they laughed together.

DEVOTIONAL GUIDE 54

"Jesus, I want to be intimate with You and Father. I want to walk in Your presence 24/7 all the days of my life. I want to have nothing hidden from You. I desire for my life to be one that converses with You, enjoys You, and releases You to others. Show me how to love others when they don't see my heart of love and when they react abusively. I need help, Jesus."

"What you have just requested, My love, is truly a narrow-road-tension that only the Holy Spirit can help you navigate. However, He delights to do so. His job is to reveal Father's plan and unpack My provision on the cross for all of your life. You have everything you need to gain your full inheritance and victory and to give Me My inheritance through you. The Holy Spirit may use revelatory insight from Father's table, or He may use someone else with whom He wants you to experience community. Either way, it is a win-win walk.

"Even though there are no formulas or steps, there are truths from which to direct your walk with Me. My words written down in Psalm 85:10 is an excellent guide: *'Mercy and loving-kindness and truth have met together; righteousness and peace have kissed each other.'*

"Walking in relationships with others is a gift...but is also hard work at times. It is Father's heart for you to share truth with mercy flowing from your heart. He wants you to walk in peace while also walking in righteousness. This is quite a balance. Every person's personality and gifts affect their wrestle to leave old ways and walk in My ways. People naturally lean one direction or another. They have a greater heart for truth or a greater heart for mercy. They have a greater heart for peace or a greater heart for righteousness. Learning your spiritual gifts and personality traits will help you know which way you need to allow Me to bring balance within you, allowing truth and mercy to meet and peace and righteousness to kiss. When you are responding to another, whether they are abusive or not, use these guidelines.

"A person who loves the truth can easily speak in a way that causes pain. If it is easy for you to see and speak the truth, guard your heart to see if you are combining your truth with loving-kindness. Otherwise your truth could wrongly cut others, producing wounds. If you simply want to 'straighten the other person out' or 'fix them,' wait until you desire My best for them. My best stems from a heart of love wanting one to know the truth because I recognize the truth will set them free. Before you speak truth to those around you, your heart needs to be broken, desiring healing and wholeness for the other person.

"Next, beware of sacrificing righteousness for peace. We want to live peaceably with others as much as possible, but never at the expense of righteousness. If you run from conflict and simply become a peace keeper rather than a peace maker, you are not cooperating with My image being formed in you and others. A peace keeper sacrifices honesty, integrity, righteousness, and the health of another's soul and their own for immediate peace. Actually you are not seeing My way of love as good for them. You may be trying to get approval from them or your own identity. If this is true, you are lying to them and not helping them to be who I created them to be. Walking through these land mines to bring wholeness to your soul and theirs is hard work and demands you love Me more than seeking to gain your identity or approval through others. Remember, truth will set you free. It simply needs to be administered through true love, not a desire to be right or to set someone straight. To be free, a person must have truth! Although it may feel like you are hurting them, you are truly giving them an opportunity to live the life I have provided.

"The Message Bible describes Psalm 85:10-13 in a wonderful way: *'Love and Truth meet in the street, Right Living and Whole Living embrace and kiss! Truth sprouts green from the ground, Right Living pours down from the skies! Oh yes! GOD gives Goodness and Beauty; our land responds with Bounty and Blessing. Right Living strides out before him, and clears a path for his passage.'* That is worth living for, isn't it My love?"

"Yes it is, Jesus. This is the life with You that I choose."

(Ponder the following Scriptures asking the Holy Spirit to open the eyes of your heart to what He wants you to presently embrace: Psalm 85:10-13; John 14:21-28; 16:7-11; Romans 12:14-21; and Ephesians 1:18. Write down your nuggets of truth. Allow them to become your very own by walking in them.)

 My Garden Within

_____

_____

_____

"You see, Ally, My desire is to reproduce Myself to the world. And I do so through you and the rest of My children. I want to set Myself on display through you, to give evidence of or demonstrate My love, My grace, My goodness, and My power to the world through you and other vessels I have made."

He stood, pulled her closer, turned her around to face outward with His hands on her shoulders, and said, "I want to present you to the world and say, 'Look, here is My daughter, made in My image. She will give evidence of Me, and by My presence within her, she will demonstrate My love, My character, and My likeness to the world.'"

Ally looked over her shoulder at Jesus and smiled.

"It's a time of presentation, Ally—to present My chosen ones to the world, to those around them. And this is a very specific time for a presentation of Me, saying of you, 'This is My daughter.' Now walk in it."

Ally was amazed at Him in her. She literally felt as if He were in her— His very life living her life.

"That's because it *is* Me, Ally."

She put her hand over her heart and took a deep breath. *Oh yeah, He knows all my thoughts.*

"At this table, and in your garden, We are making you into a vessel of honor. When you are here, you are cultivating a friendship with Me and with the Father. Come to this table of revelation often, and We will pour into your vessel everything needed for your journey. Let Me see your stones," He said, holding out His hand.

Ally reached into her pocket and pulled out her little pouch of stones. She handed it to Jesus.

He poured them out on the table and picked up the little black stone, the first one He had presented her with. "Do you remember your dark but comely stone?" He held it out for her to take. "Do you know what makes you comely to Me? Lovely to Me? It is not in your performance, Ally; your loveliness is found in the image of Me and in a willing heart that longs for Me. You were created to be like Me. You were destined from the beginning to be molded into the image of the Son and share inwardly My likeness."

Ally grabbed a little pink vessel from a shelf and put her small fist inside it. She felt the smoothness of its interior as she spoke, saying, "I want to be like You on the inside."

Jesus smiled wide and said, "In the garden of your soul, as you spend time with the Gardener, Me, I will fashion your insides to be like Me, as well as the outside. I will change your countenance and your behaviors. We will fashion your life to resemble Ours."

Ally stood up and began twirling and dancing, and said, "So others will say of me, 'She looks just like her heavenly Father.'"

⇜ DEVOTIONAL GUIDE 55 ⇝

"Jesus, I want with all my heart to be a vessel of honor for You. I don't want to be argumentative, doing it my way, but to be a gentle listener and a teacher who keeps her cool when others don't seem to get it. I want to be a vessel of honor enabling others to come to their senses and escape out of the trap in which the enemy is holding them captive. However, it seems I mess it up more than I help. Can You give me some insights as to how to do it better?"

"With great delight, My love," Jesus answered, "The first point to remember is you may not do it perfectly but you will not do it wrong when you trust Me the best you know how. Our journey is a love walk. I can take all things and work them together for good for those who love Me and are fitting into My plans.

"Relationship with Me and others is a pivotal way I use to expose weaknesses in order to change them into strengths thereby revealing My image. Let Me give you some truths with which to work:

- Work your way out of living a performance-based life. No walking on egg shells. Such a life is destructive.

- Do not assume responsibility for another's life. Only assume responsibility for staying in My presence and saying and responding how I lead you to speak and respond. I will take it from there.

- When you feel like arguing, seeking to convince, defending yourself or blaming, take a deep breath and wait patiently with Me until you have My mind and heart.

- Take my mother's advice given in John 2:5, 'Whatever He says to you, do it.'

- Sometimes My Spirit-inspired words will pierce the darkness in another as you firmly challenge negative, disrespectful, or barbed words. Your words need to be firm but kind.

- Some situations will call for you to look firmly, but not harshly at the one spewing hurtful words, but say nothing.

- Other times you will need to evaluate, pray silently, or give a blessing. I know the other person's needs. My resources are unlimited. You may be amazed at times what I say through you.

"In conclusion, My love, remember you are not to become polluted or lose your peace to sustain the life of another. Sustaining life is My job! Your job is to stay in My presence."

"Thank You, Jesus. These thoughts give me peace and direction with which to trust You."

(Take your time reading the following Scriptures, trusting the Holy Spirit to show what you need to see at this point in your journey: Proverbs 27:17; Romans 12:14; and 2 Timothy 2:19-26. Record your conclusions. Return to each thought until you have assimilated what He is showing you.)

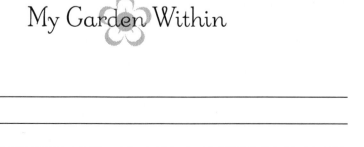

My Garden Within

Jesus was thrilled to see her taking on the shape and form He planned for her.

"Your loveliness and beauty came from the gift of righteousness that became yours when you first believed in Me."

She continued to twirl; she had so much joy, just like a little girl who found out she was really a princess. "I am lovely because of what You did for me, not what I do for You. For I have a loving King"—she curtsied before Him—"who gave away His beauty to take away my ugliness and insecurities. It is through Your sacrifice that I am made lovely and beautiful in Your sight."

He enjoyed watching the dance of her life. "Ally, that day when you turned to Me, and said yes to Me, the work of the Holy Spirit made you lovely in My sight. I want you to know that I do not see you in your weakness, but rather I see My grace inside your heart. I see the beauty of My life forming within you."

He pulled her to Him, knelt before her, and placed His hands on her stomach. "You see, you possess inside you, in the most secret and hidden places of your heart, your garden, your life, beautiful virtues that will one day be seen by all. You won't be able to contain them, because you will be so full of Me. Right now they may be just seeds, those things I have planted in you, those dreams, those visions. If you continue to water and tend to your garden, if you continue to let the Gardener work in you, in time those seeds will spring up into magnificent beauty for your Bridegroom. This image, My image, is growing in you, being fashioned in you, and reflecting back to Me and to those who surround you. I see the beauty of My life being formed in your eyes."

"Today, Lord," Ally said, "I am transformed by Your extravagant love!" She put both of her hands over her heart and said, "The day will come when my garden will be so refreshing and my life will not be lived to impress others, but will become the overflow of Your life living in me. For You are truly living inside me, and You are making me into a vessel of honor, to pour Your life into others."

With that, she spun with her face lifted high and found herself back in her small plot of land in her earthly garden. And there on the ground before her, where the crushed dahlia had been, was that little pink vessel she had held back at her Father's table. Inside was a small, folded note.

When she unfolded it, a beautiful purple stone fell out. She heard His voice in her heart say, "Royalty. Purple stands for royalty." Again she felt like a princess. She looked at the note, which had clearly come from Jesus; it read, "You look just like your heavenly Father."

DEVOTIONAL GUIDE 56

"Jesus, because of Your extravagant love I am being made into a vessel of honor. It is almost too good to be true. I not only want to see myself as You see me, but I also want to see others with whom I am not reconciled with Your eyes. At times, it seems so hopeless. Please shine Your light upon my heart."

"With much delight, My love, I will share some nuggets with you. It is important you know the difference between forgiveness and reconciliation. As I explained earlier, forgiveness is a one-way street between you and Me. However, reconciliation is a two-way street. You can reach out your hand to people, but they may not be ready to reach out their hands to you. The time of reconciliation may come later...or not at all.

"If you are aware of having offended someone, you who are more mature should take the first step to apologize for any wrong you have done. Notice, I said a wrong you have done, not what the person perceives you have done. Don't create an apology or assume responsibility for something for which you are not responsible. Should you reach out to the person and a fury of anger or flares of accusations and condemnation are released, you know that he or she is not ready for reconciliation. Gently back off.

"Depending upon the situation, you may say you are sorry for the conflict between you. You may agree to disagree and move forward on any grounds of equality you can settle upon. However, if that is not possible, you humbly wait upon Me, allowing Me to work where you cannot.

"In the meantime, guard your heart against hardness and cultivate tender affection toward them, releasing them into My hands. Any door that is opened, walk through carefully, allowing Me to direct your steps. You can trust My extravagant love for them…just as you have My extravagant love for you.

"John Wesley, the founder of Methodism, made a statement that has helped many in similar situations. 'You are under no obligation to think of him anymore, except when you commend him to God in prayer. You need not speak of him anymore, but leave him to his own Master. Indeed, you still owe to him, as to all other heathens, tender goodwill. You owe him courtesy and civility, but not friendship.'

"The last nugget is to faithfully strip off your old ways of responding from your carnal heart and put on your new nature from the heart I gave you. As I am living in and through you, you will be a vessel of honor, opening a window for others to be drawn to Me."

"Jesus, You are so wonderful! I love learning to trust You and my heavenly Father. Thanks for Your patience with me."

(Meditate upon Jesus' words written in 2 Corinthians 5:12-21, Matthew 5:21-26, Ephesians 4:22-24, and 2 Timothy 2:20-21. Let the words sink deeply into the garden of your soul. Record your response.)

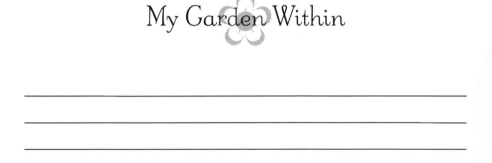

My Garden Within

_____

_____

_____

Devotional Guide Inventory Chapter 12

1. Why do many people fear our heavenly Father? Why does the enemy seek to separate you from your heavenly Father? Why does an authority figure misrepresent Father's heart? Who drew you to Jesus? How do you know what Father is like? Why?

2. Who is involved in the act of forgiveness? How is forgiveness and trust different? How is real love shown in regard to another person's wrong behavior? What are consequences suffered for wrong actions designed to accomplish? What does drinking the spikenard represent in your Christian walk?

3. What does truth need to be joined with before it is spoken? What happens if truth and loving-kindness are not present? What is the difference between being a peace keeper and a peace maker? What result according to Psalm 85:10-13 do we gain from doing it God's way?

4. When you are being a vessel of honor, whose life is your responsibility? When you feel like arguing, defending, or blaming, what should you do? What are some ways you may respond to people who are abusive to help them come to their senses? Which applies to your present situation and gives you direction?

5. How is reconciliation different from forgiveness? For what are you to apologize? How can you tell if the other person is open for reconciliation? When the person with whom you are seeking reconciliation is arguing, defending, or blaming, what does that tell you about his or her present readiness for reconciliation? If

the other person is not ready for reconciliation, what do you do? Until reconciliation is accomplished, what must you carefully guard? Why? Does John Wesley's statement help you know how to navigate this painful situation? How?

My Garden Within Inventory

CHAPTER 13

I Will Change Your Name

He knows my name, what He calls me, when we commune with Him, He reveals who we really are. He who is able to hear, let him listen to and heed what the Spirit says. To him who overcomes, I will give to eat of the manna that is hidden, I will give him a white stone with a new name engraved on the stone, which no one knows or understands except he who receives it (see Revelation 2:17).

The following morning, Ally awoke early, hearing the voice she was coming to know so well speak to her heart.

"And you shall be called by a new name, which the mouth of the Lord shall name, and this new name that I have for you is who you really are."

Ally grew excited to get up and spend some time at the table she'd visited the day before to understand what these words meant. She showered, made herself a dry cappuccino drizzled with caramel, her favorite, and sat down in her big leather chair. She grabbed her Bible and asked with great anticipation, "What do You call me, Lord?"

Suddenly she found herself not in her garden, but in a garden far more beautiful and far more colorful than she had ever even imagined. It was teeming with life—actually, it was *breathing life*. It was occupied with brilliant flowers that surrounded her and that she knew did not grow on the earth. The colors of this place were beyond her own vocabulary. Vibrant was the only word she could think of.

Could it be, she thought, *that this is a garden in heaven?*

"Exactly."

She turned to see Jesus. He looked a bit different from when she had seen Him in her own garden. He looked kingly and simply dignified, and the light that shone around Him was almost blinding.

"Did I die?" Ally asked apprehensively.

Jesus laughed. "No, We just wanted to bring you here today, to Eden, because We want to give you something from here."

Ally was astonished at her surroundings—almost like an animated movie. All the flowers appeared to be alive—alive like humans, with personality and character. She realized that she couldn't even put her thoughts into words to describe the beauty in which she found herself.

"We want to give you a new name."

Oh my goodness, Ally thought as she remembered the Word she had woken up to.

"The new name that You have for me will reveal who I really am, right?"

DEVOTIONAL GUIDE 57

"Jesus, what You call me is who I really am, I am coming to realize. I am excited about knowing my new name from You. However, for my identity to be established necessitates having what I have depended on to be shaken off. For instance, when I have depended upon another's approval and I get rejection, I get confused and everything feels chaotic. My soul is learning to be dependent on my human spirit via the Holy Spirit, but when the confusion and chaos begin I often get overwhelmed. Can You help me know how to ride through this storm of being established in my new name?"

Jesus smiled His warm smile that always settles and brings peace to my soul. He said, "Even though I have synchronized your soul with your human spirit, it does take time for the healing to settle in and stabilization to be established. I have written down in My Word, in Matthew 18:18, some truths about binding and loosing that I want you to use to do your part to bring about wholeness.

"Whether it is before falling asleep at night or during the day when there is chaos from ordinary living, say the following: 'With my heart or human spirit I look full into Father's face receiving my present portion of grace for my every need according to Your ordained plan. Soul, I bind your will to Father's will. Mind, I bind you to the mind of Christ. Emotions, I bind you to the Holy Spirit for healing, comfort, and alignment with godly emotions. From my soul I loose, break, and trample upon every proud and lofty thing set up against the true knowledge of God. Body, I bind you to the will of God to fulfill His destiny purposes.'

"As you do your part of binding and loosing, enter into My rest knowing I will be working within your inner garden changing you from the inside out. Remember, My beloved, success comes not from trying harder but receiving from Me what you cannot do on your own as you give Me your consent to work within. That is My grace.

"As you continue to move from surviving to thriving, trust the Holy Spirit to expose any hidden fears, lies, and performance imbedded within the inner garden of your soul. Immediately, give them to Me and I will remove as only I can. Each removal leaves more room for Me to fill you with Myself, making you fully alive!

"I bless your soul to discern the voice of the Holy Spirit who will never leave you and receive your much needed rest and new assignment."

"Jesus, thank You so much. I am excited about my new name. I know it will help me realize the loving patience with which You have guided my life. I love You so much!"

(Carefully study the following Scriptures asking the Holy Spirit to open the eyes of your heart to absorb all you can receive at this time: Matthew 18:18; 1 Corinthians 2:16; 2 Corinthians 10:5, Matthew 11:28-30; Ephesians 4:7. Record your thoughts and meditate upon them until they are yours.)

My Garden Within

Jesus was thrilled because He knew that her spirit had heard His voice that morning as she lay in bed.

"Yes, I want to tell you what We call you. Many of Our children will not receive or know their new name until they get here, to heaven. But there are a few to whom We reveal their new names earlier so as to mold them into the character of that name while they are still on the earth. It is to shape them, so to speak, for their work on the earth."

Ally's mind went to the ones whose names God changed in the Scriptures, so what He was telling her was beginning to make sense. Her excitement grew to hear this new name.

"Peter, Jacob, Sarah, and Abraham are ones you have heard of, right?" Jesus asked. Then, seeing her nod, He continued, "But did you know about these? Joshua, Paul, Barnabas, Barsabbas, Thaddaeus, or Mark? And then there were James and John, I liked to call those two *Boanerges,* which means "Sons of Thunder." I renamed them all! You see, I enjoy naming My children; it makes them who they really are, who I created them to be. It reveals to them their true identity."

Ally was still astonished by her surroundings, but more so by Jesus and the brightness of His countenance.

"In obedience, as you begin to use your new name, you will see a change immediately. For your character will change, and your demeanor will change." He noticed Ally's expression as she tried to remember what that word *demeanor* meant.

"The way you act," He explained, smiling.

"Got it." Ally nodded.

He continued, "Even your countenance will change—the way you look, both to yourself and to others."

Ally smiled at Him.

DEVOTIONAL GUIDE 58

"Jesus, as You changed Abraham, Paul, and the others' names, was their ability to walk in their new name immediate or gradual?"

Jesus understood the tendency to want instant change and the enemy's trap seeking any means to disappoint His beloved. He said with a special tenderness, "My beloved, thank you for bringing up this point. It took Abraham awhile to wrap his mind around the fact he was the father of nations. Paul stayed in Arabia for a period of time to adjust his zeal to My plan and name for him rather than his old zeal. Remember, I have shared that change is gradual, enabling you to not lose touch with who I am in you and who you are in Me. You have cooperated so beautifully and I am so proud of you. I am the Cornerstone of your life. Pulling away the wrongly laid stones and building again is a process. If you please, it is cyclical. Tearing down and rebuilding according to My time table doesn't create new trauma.

"Let's review a little to put it all in perspective. Even though the decision has been made for your human spirit, soul, and body to be properly aligned, adjustment time is required. For instance, when you feel the need to rise up to protect yourself, remember My protection is trustworthy. When you begin to panic wanting to think of a solution, intentionally submit to My mind. When your emotions feel like they are about to explode, run to Me and rest in My presence. Remind yourself I am here to heal the broken places in your heart. I hold all things together within you, in deepest heaven and on earth.

"It will take time for the old ways of surviving to be dismantled and the alignment receiving the Holy Spirit's flow to become the way of life. I am accomplishing your new name revealed in you as fast as is expedient. The Holy Spirit will give you insight enabling you to cooperate with Me. You simply flow with Him."

"Jesus, walking with You, watching my new name be released is exciting. I am so glad You know what You are doing. I trust in You!"

(Meditate upon the following Scriptures trusting the Holy Spirit to bring them alive for your present need: Genesis 17:1-6; Galatians 1:11-18; Psalm 68; Luke 4:18-19; and Isaiah 28:16. Write down what comforts you. Dwell upon it.)

My Garden Within

_____

_____

_____

Jesus pressed on, "You see, this new name will bring you out of the captivity you have been in, and it will give you a new view of yourself. For example, I doubt that Sarai, whom you know as Sarah in the Bible, saw herself as a princess, which is what Sarah means. She needed to see herself differently. By giving her a new name, I began the process of helping her to see herself in a new way. She began to take on the characteristics of that new name and therefore was made into another image, the image of whom I said she was. It was the same for her husband, Abram, whom I named Abraham, the father of many nations. Each time their names were spoken by other people, their futures were being prophesied or changed to fulfill their destiny. I remade them and refashioned them, just like you saw Me do to that vessel on the wheel yesterday. Changing their names began that process.

"I am also shaping you, Ally. I have a new place for you, and every time people call you by your new name, they will be prophesying who you really are, and that will shape your future."

Ally's anticipation continued to grow, and she smiled at Jesus.

"I can transform lives in many ways, but one way that I love is to do it by changing names."

"Won't people think I'm weird?"

"They already do." Jesus nudged her, and they laughed together.

"But in all seriousness, here's the thing, Ally—if you are obedient and you do this, if you go by this new name, the process will deliver you from the opinions of others."

Ally thought about that statement; she had lived most of her life worrying about what people thought about her. *Oh, to be free from that would be amazing.*

DEVOTIONAL GUIDE 59

"Thank You, Jesus, for patiently and lovingly working with me to separate the impurities either done to me or by me in order to reveal my new name and identity. I am seeing that my identity in You is the core of my stability and peace. Thank You, for I know that my new name will reflect Your passionate heart of love. Now that my soul and human spirit are aligned and being stabilized, is there anything I can do to help my body?"

Jesus said with His tender heart for healing revealed, "Truly My ways are far above your ways and My thoughts above your thoughts. I work in many different ways. However, let me share a technique or tool many of My Body is using that will give aid in synchronizing your body with your soul and spirit. Your brain had to adjust to the survival season of your soul. You may instruct your brain, the control center of your body, to take its rightful place reflecting your new name in unity with your soul and spirit. The following prayer is a guide. Allow the Holy Spirit to guide, adding and implementing as He leads. When you use this technique, think of it as My hands on your head and forehead. Remember, I laid hands on the sick, and they recovered.

"Place your left hand on the top of your head on the wide bundle of connectors that connect the left brain and the right brain. It is called the corpus callosum and facilitates the communication between the two hemispheres. Place one or more of your right fingers on the forehead.

"Pray: 'Father, align the left brain and the right brain into its optimal functioning as You designed it through the corpus callosum. Align spirit, soul, and body with the Father, Son, and Holy Spirit in three-fold alignment.'

"Bless: 'I bless myself with alignment of spirit, soul, and body with the Father, Son, and Holy Spirit in three-fold agreement.'

"Receive: Stay with it, and remind yourself to receive, not pray, just receive. Thank Me for alignment of spirit, soul, and body with the Father, Son, and Holy Spirit in three-fold agreement. Listen and see what I am saying or doing. There is often a manifestation of heat in either the top of the head or the forehead, but not always. That's good but not necessary. Just stay in receiving mode for two or three minutes, or until I say I am done.

"Do this for yourself when you feel off-kilter or if you are facing something important for increased sense of strength and focus.

"Continue with this statement speaking to your brain, 'Now, Brain, you have habitually referred to the past in making decisions. I charge you now to look to the Kingdom of God within you as you make decisions for now and the future.' Bring forth the Kingdom of God within you into your present; enjoy being who Father created you to be. Prophesy to yourself, that the Kingdom of God is yours now and is coming into the earth realm as His and your reality. This expedites bringing the Kingdom of heaven into the Kingdom of God on earth and into your life. Conclude by quoting Psalm 68:1, '*Let God arise and His enemies be scattered.*'

"Just a gentle reminder, My beloved, changing a habit typically takes at least twenty-one days. Changes in the body often take longer. Don't be discouraged."

"Jesus, You amaze me with Your extravagant love. I love You. Thank You for revealing to me my new name."

(Write what you see in the following Scriptures: 3 John 2; Isaiah 53:3-5; 55:8-9; Psalm 68:1; Luke 17:21. Praise Him for His work when you can see it and when you cannot. Record your praise.)

My Garden Within

_____

_____

_____

It was then she asked, "What do You call me?"

Jesus smiled and walked over to her. He pulled up a lily that was dancing on the hillside, handed it to her, and said, "Zoe. We call you Zoe."

The instant she heard the name, peace flooded her soul, and it brought an immediate confidence in the fact that He had changed her name.

"This is a descriptive name," He continued. "I want to transmit to you a mental image of who you really are, who We made you to be."

"Zoe," she said, pondering the name.

"You are going to be one who helps others become whole. You will help them to live again, to truly live the abundant life that I came to give them. Do you realize that this is what I have been teaching you in the garden of your soul and in this Garden of Eden?"

She thought back on all that He had taught her.

"You have heard and watched Me teach truths to you, and you have changed. Now I entrust you to pass these revelations and insights down to others so they will grow into all I have for them and will themselves teach others. You see, I have been molding you for a life-giving purpose. I will cause you to flourish, and this is what I see: I see you walking by others' gardens, which will begin to flourish instantly. I am giving you not only a brand-new name, but also a brand-new life. My life in you will change you and others."

She already felt a new vibrancy inside. The new name was life-giving.

"Do you remember when we first entered your garden, Zoe?"

He called me Zoe, she thought, feeling more change.

"How it looked to be dead and like all life was gone?"

"Ah, yes, how could I forget?" she replied.

"There are many broken people in the world and even in your life now. Things or circumstances came into their lives, whether through their own choosing or not, which devastated their lives. Whether self-inflicted or otherwise, they feel forsaken, lost, and dead. They feel lost and think they are desolate and without hope—just like you felt."

Her heart saddened. She knew exactly what that felt like, for she had experienced that very thing.

"I want to come into their lives just as I came into yours. I want to replace their mourning with joy. I want to restore the years the enemy has taken and rebuild the places he destroyed, leaving them feeling desolate and alone. I want to give them life."

Zoe thought again about the condition of her soul when they first entered her garden.

"As you give what you've been given, as you live and walk in Me, it will cause others to want to walk in Me and live in Me also."

She drew in her breath, and held it while she smiled.

"I gave you life, Zoe. Now give it away." As He said this, He handed her a white, polished stone, and across it, one word was written.

Zoe

~DEVOTIONAL GUIDE 60~

"Jesus, I'm excited to know that as I walk in Your presence, my new name is being established, releasing the ministry You have planned. If I knew what it was, I would probably seek to monitor myself by that name to try to help You produce it. What can You tell me to help in this area?"

Jesus smiled with delight as He said, "My beloved, you are understanding yourself very well. My Bride has often been misled by the enemy by reversing the proper order of her ministry and her identity or new name.

Your ministry is important but it must flow from knowing your identity or you will be deceived and hit walls that are harmful. In other words, you would have been doing step two, your ministry, before you had your foundation or step one of who I am in you established. It's like trying to drive a car without gasoline. The car is important but you need gasoline. You can push the car, tow the car, or drag the car, but it is not operating as effectively as the designer planned. When you know who I am in you, the resources never end because I am your identity and supply. Reversing the order, you make who you are in Me more important than who I am in you—subtle but strategic. The enemy is subtle!

"You see, roles change in families, careers, ministries, and other areas in which you live, but I never change. I will not forsake you. I am your life, not just what you are doing! When there is shaking or rearranging in these areas, you simply settle into Me, drink from My living water, and move forward as I lead you. The shaking or rearranging simply repositions you for a broader assignment. What needs to fall off does, and what is good finds its place building your godly character.

"Think of John. My disciple's words about himself describes a time when I was with him on earth. '*There was leaning on Jesus' bosom one of His disciples, whom Jesus loved,*' according to John 13:23 (NKJV). As you continue to walk in My presence, it is like leaning on My bosom hearing My heartbeat of love for you. Nothing can shake you in this place of living. Your new name will be fully revealed in My time and in My way."

Jesus' eyes sparkled with a divine brightness as He spoke. "Yes, My beloved, you understand and receive your new name with each act of obedience, saying about yourself what I say. Each time you speak the truth about yourself even when and especially when you don't feel it; your identity has a growth spurt! The new name I have for you I have breathed My life into. Remember, I am the last Adam who became the life-giving Spirit. I and only I give life!"

"Jesus, thank You for how You have made me. Thank You for my assignment. I shall listen to Your voice and obey You and give what You have given to me to others. Life is good! My eyes are upon You, focusing upon who You are in me. How exciting to live as You lead."

(Meditate upon John 13:23; 1 Corinthians 15:35-47; Philippians 4:19; and Psalm 139:13-18. Ponder His words to you.)

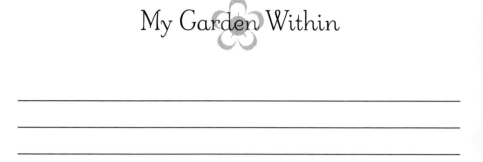

My Garden Within

_____

_____

_____

Devotional Guide Inventory Chapter 13

1. What is an exercise you can do according to Matthew 18:18 when confusing, chaotic and overwhelming feelings seek to overtake you? How does this work in synchronizing the spirit, soul, and body? Once you have bound and loosened, what should be your next step? How are you learning to enter into His rest or peace? What is your part? How does the removal of fears, lies, and performance affect your soul and your capacity to be more fully alive in Jesus?

2. Is change usually instant or gradual? Why? Who is your Cornerstone? What is your part when wrongly laid stones are being torn down? How do you cooperate with His rebuilding process?

3. Is the body affected by your surviving techniques, which have eliminated God from the process? What tool can you use to realign the body, especially the brain, to divine alignment? What is to be the new focus for the brain in moving forward? How long does it often take to change a habit? How long for changes in the body?

4. From whom does your identity or new name come? What is a subtle deception the enemy would use to try to trap you? What changes and what doesn't in regard to daily living life? How do you remain stable in your identity? Who breathes into your new name bringing it to life?

My Garden Within Inventory

_____

_____

_____

_____

_____

_____

_____

_____

_____

_____

_____

_____

_____

_____

_____

_____

_____

_____

_____

_____

_____

_____

CHAPTER 14

Fruit

...with Me [God] is the fruit found [which is to nourish you]
(Hosea 14:8).

It is a joy to Jesus when a person takes time to walk more
intimately with Him. The bearing of fruit is always shown in
Scripture to be a visible result of an intimate relationship with
Jesus Christ. –Oswald Chambers[1]

"Give life away." Those words hung in Zoe's mind as she walked through the rest of her day, clutching the white stone with her new name written across it.

"In knowing Me, you become like Me."

She heard His voice as if He were standing right in the room with her. She had spent the day getting some things done around her house. She had also meditated on the time she'd spent that morning in the secret place—this time, in the Garden of Eden with her beloved Jesus. And once again, He was conversing with her.

"It's much more than knowing about Me."

Zoe was immediately in her garden again, this time surrounded by an orchard of apple trees. *His voice is coming from up inside one of these trees,* she thought, and she continued to follow the sound. She then looked up into one of the trees and saw His feet dangling down.

He lowered down a basket filled with apples from a little pulley that He had rigged to get the apples from high in the tree to the ground without bruising them.

Zoe grabbed the basket as it got closer to her and set it gently on the ground.

"Again, I can't say this enough—it is about spending time with Me here in the secret place, the garden of your soul." He began to climb down the tree toward her. "It's getting to know My love for you, My mercy, and My character in very personal and real ways."

He took the final jump out of the tree and stood right before her. "This is eternal life—that you would know Me and also that you would know our Father who sent Me to the world. This is how I lived on the earth: in constant fellowship with Him. And I want you to have constant and continuing fellowship with Me. I know that is how you will produce lots of life-giving fruit." He reached down and picked up the full basket of apples on the ground. "Knowing Me and living this life in Me produces much fruit that will nourish lives wherever you go."

"So this fruit is a visible result of intimacy with You?" Zoe reached down and pulled an apple from the basket.

"Yes," He responded, "with the purpose of showing the Father fully on the earth. Live in the Spirit every day, always aware of what He is doing and saying in every situation, and then join Him in the work that He has for you on the earth. This takes intimate time spent in the secret place."

DEVOTIONAL GUIDE 61

"Jesus, I do not want to miss any part of my eternal life with You—now or forever. I want to know You, not just about You. I want to know Your love, mercy, and character in a very personal and real way. Please share with me any stumbling block that could slow down my process of knowing You."

Jesus was so thrilled to talk about this ingredient. With His special smile His words began to flow, "My very special beloved Bride, there is nothing closer to My heart than you knowing not only Me, but My love, mercy, goodness, and character. The road to fully living life with Me means doing what many are not willing to do. However, I can see your heart and know you not only want the truth, but you will also walk with Me in My truth to be truly free...fully alive.

"Pain! Many spend their lives trying to avoid pain and not cooperating with My healing process. I am not the source of pain. The enemy brought pain into the Garden of Eden when Adam and Eve yielded to his temptation. They believed him not Me. However, I have now conquered sin and death that were meant to destroy My precious creation—you! As you embrace the pain, either brought on by your wrong choices or others, and walk with Me through the healing process, you will experience My love, mercy, goodness, and character as released through My death on the cross for you.

"Be aware, My beloved Bride, unresolved trauma from childhood can leave you with internal states that are separated from each other and often in conflict with each other. Your individual pain may have different manifestations than someone else's. If you were severely wounded, this part may have been hidden to protect you until healing comes. Any shame, fear, or despair coming from this hidden part is not your fault. Neither is feeling ugly, stupid, or worthless. 'I deserve what I got and no one could possibly love me,' is a lie coming from the evil one who abused you.

"If you have become negative, judging yourself and others, seeking to remain in charge because you haven't learned to trust Me, let's turn the tables on the enemy. Be willing to be compassionate to yourself, fully receiving the love I bring to you through others. Or nurture yourself by speaking My words written down to you until you believe them within. This may be very hard until you receive My love, grace, and compassion from others and allow the Holy Spirit to comfort you. Most of all invite Me into your pain and ask Me what I want you to know about the situation or My heart concerning what happened. I may give you a picture, a thought, or words through others. Know I care and am working. The answer may come later even in a dream or some other time or way.

"As you embrace the pain—not being paralyzed by it, letting it make you a victim, or forming your identity—there will be times you will feel like you are going to die. I will be holding you in My righteous right hand unlocking the doors to the prisons that have held the pain. You can trust Me. Let *Me* be your God, not your pain or your feelings, but the truth that I am here and will never forsake you. We are partners gaining freedom My way!

"You and I together are birthing My image into you. You are discovering your identity in Me. You are living out your new name. Carefully read My words written down to you and embrace them knowing I give only good gifts."

"Jesus, You are right. I will trust You because I know Your ways are for my good. Thank You for being my strength as I embrace pain, knowing You are My redeemer, My healer! I am looking forward to the day when I can say that there is no pain this life can throw at me that can put out the fire of my love for You."

(Carefully and prayerfully read Psalms 145:7-9; 34:8; John 16:21, 33; Galatians 4:19; and Isaiah 41:10. Write down what comes to your mind.)

My Garden Within

Zoe began to polish the apple on her pants.

"Intimacy with God, the Father, Me, and the Holy Spirit always produces fruit, life, and nourishment—not only for you, but also for others."

She held the apple to her face and saw her reflection in its glossy surface. She then set her gaze back on Jesus.

"You see, Our desire is for everyone who believes to be fruitful. That was the plan from the very beginning: to be fruitful and to multiply. Our heart is that your lives and your gardens would germinate life in you and in all that you do."

"Germinate?" she questioned.

"To cause growth, to sprout, to begin to grow. To plant seeds in others. We want you to live a life that causes others to want that same life—a life of intimacy."

Zoe thought back on her conversation with her friends at the coffee shop. After she had shared her heart about her Beloved, and after they had watched her countenance change before them, they too wanted what she had.

"That is the spirit of multiplication…when others see and taste of the fruit you share, they will want their own fruit."

Zoe's mind went back to who she had been and the change that spending time with Jesus brought. "I know for me"—she looked at Him—"I had to surrender who I was, my old unrenewed self. That true surrender and vulnerability to You brought intimacy with You. You loved me in my renewed state because You saw the potential of Your life in me."

Jesus smiled at her, and touched her cheek. "And that intimacy produced fruit in you, Zoe, and that fruit causes multiplication."

"Be fruitful and multiply," Zoe said. "Your fruit causes others to want what nourishes the soul, the mind, and the heart. Seeing your fruit in me causes people to want You. For Your fruit brings life—a life filled with love, joy, peace, patience, faithfulness, goodness, kindness, gentleness, and self-control."

As Zoe heard again the fruit that comes from the very heart and Spirit of God, she began to see in her own life the abundance of the fruit that she knew came only from spending intimate time with the lover of her soul.

DEVOTIONAL GUIDE 62

"Jesus, my heart longs to release the spirit of multiplication originating in the Garden of Eden to be taken to others. However, there is a problem I don't understand. I am observing the same destructive patterns in me and my physical family continuing to multiple. How can I stop ungodly multiplication?"

"My beloved Bride, you are growing in wisdom, understanding, and hungering for truth. I am so proud of you. As you are observing, I will never bruise the fruit in your life. It is obvious you are ready for another very important insight.

"The enemy often leaves his trail of destruction within families. You do not have to follow them. However, there is often a weakness or drawing to certain behaviors you have had modeled or an internal drawing to repeat destructive behaviors.

"Often as believers grow to maturity and observe destructive patterns in the lives of their family, they vow to never become like the ungodly behavior they observe. Such a conclusion seems wise on the surface, however only I have the power to break sin and death, the cause of pain. If you seek to accomplish good behavior in your own strength, the evil will simply take another form. Actually, you have become a god unto yourself, which My word calls an idol.

"Making such a vow can drive you subconsciously in a destructive way. The good news is when you see this truth you can turn from trusting yourself to trusting Me. Repentance is the word. Daniel's example in My Word in Daniel chapter 9 describes identification repentance. Daniel identified with his people. He repented for the sins of his people as if they were his own sins, as well as assuming responsibility for his own sins. You are to do the same. In some ways you may have contributed to sins by cooperating even when you didn't realize what you were doing. Forgive your ancestors and yourself for the doors that were opened to ungodly patterns and contamination for your life and theirs. Forgive and release them from yourself. Renounce and break these sinful generational patterns and cycles of behavior and their power to influence your life and your generations going forward. Then ask Me to release the flood of blessings for you and your generations to come. Thank Me for releasing them now."

A detailed prayer is given in Appendix C for your consideration.

"Jesus, that makes so much sense. You are wisdom! You show me the way. You are my life. Thank You for Your love poured out on me. I will do as You have asked."

(Ponder and apply the following Scriptures: Daniel 9; Psalms 115:18; 135:15-18; and 1 John 5:21. Write down your insights and commitments for the future.)

My Gaden Within

---

"There is a very important aspect of this fruitful life, Zoe," Jesus said as He emptied the full basket of apples into a nearby cart.

He captured her attention because she had recognized in His tone that the next words from His mouth were of great worth.

"You must remain in Me. Live your life in Me. As a branch cannot bear fruit all by itself, neither can you unless you remain in Me."

He walked back up to the tree, picked up the shears that He had used earlier in her garden, and cut off a branch that was heavy with fruit. "Cut off from Me, you produce nothing. You need to stay focused on the source of true life. In all of your uncertainties and insecurities, the only guarantee for having peace in your heart and fruit in your life is to remain in My love."

He grabbed her hand, and she felt pierced in her heart as He held it. Looking into her big, brown eyes, He said, "My love surpasses all other love. My love is compassionate: it heals, forgives, and reassures. It is a love that gives you life. Being cut off from this love leaves you disheartened and disconnected, and eventually everything in you will die. Stay in Me, Zoe." As He said these last words, tears formed in His eyes and started to flow down His cheeks. He was pleading with her to stay in Him.

Why would anyone ever want to leave this kind of love? she wondered.

She reached out her hand and wiped His cheeks as her own tears now flowed from her eyes.

He so loved her heart, saying, "When you stay in Me, you become like Me; you will begin to take on My characteristics. In staying, you are conformed and transformed into My very image."

She again saw her reflection in His eyes.

DEVOTIONAL GUIDE 63

"Jesus, Your tenderness deeply touches me. I am seeing Your heart of relentless love poured out for me on the cross. However, my heart still quivers when I see the shears in Your hand. Help me, please."

Jesus' eyes continued to sparkle with the tears flowing down His cheeks from His pleading with me to stay with Him. "My beloved Bride," Jesus said, "your identity is sealed and your heart is truly joined with Mine is a deep trust. When pruning starts, remember it is designed to make you truly fruitful. Often you confuse Me with an earthly authority that has misrepresented Father's love. Earthly fathers may try. But My heavenly Father always does what is right and good for you. You can trust Him. We are fashioning you to be My Bride and His child.

"When the pruning or training seems too severe, push deeply into Me letting Me bring into reality what I have already laid hold of for you so you can experience it now. Know you are being corrected or trained in ways of holiness to reap a rich harvest for yourself and My Kingdom. No discipline may seem good at times, but keep in mind My training means you are truly Father's child and legitimate offspring. We are removing everything that doesn't look like Us, and what remains will fall into place. Don't be amazed by the shaking, training, or discipline. Be comforted you are truly loved as a true daughter.

"Our correction is to be welcomed with open arms because it yields Our likeness in you, peaceable fruit of righteousness that causes others to want Me. I kept My eyes on finishing the race while on earth. I will strengthen you to do the same. The race we are running is worth your life poured out for now and eternity. Be a long-distance runner like Me and run for it. You are living for something bigger than you…life itself! Being fully alive!"

"Thank You, Jesus. I do continue to forget I am being trained in godliness. I know Your sovereign hand will not allow anything to touch my life that is outside Your redemptive power. Thank You. I love You, Jesus."

(Ask the Holy Spirit to open your eyes to life-changing truths as you read the following Scriptures: Hebrews 12 and Philippians 3:11-16. Ponder what speaks to you as you write it down to study and review.)

My Garden Within

_____

_____

_____

"This intimacy that you are experiencing right now not only brings joy and fruitfulness, but also proves that you are being changed into My image, into My very likeness. You are becoming an extension of who I am—a shoot that, when joined with others, will fill the whole earth with My love."

Zoe again thought of her heart's condition when she had first met with Jesus, and she had an "aha moment." She looked at Him and said, "You have caused me to be fruitful in the land of my affliction. In all my hurt and pain, I spent time with You in my garden. Instead of just running to the world for help, I ran to You." Tears began to flow again. "It was there You healed me, Lord, in the secret place."

He wiped her tears, replying, "You know, before you were ever born, I knew your journey, and I knew the fruit that would be birthed and find its home in you because of that journey. It was your journey to wholeness."

Zoe nodded.

"Some of the things you went through were tough, really hard things, but you now have fruit to share with others who have gone through some of those things, to help them and to nourish them back into wholeness."

Jesus grabbed a nearby hose, attached it to a deep-root-watering device, and pushed it into the ground at the base of one of her trees in the orchard. It would provide the tree's root system with water.

"I am your keeper, and I have been watering you every moment of your life. I have been watering with a strong purpose for your life—that my truths would take root and change your life and that your life would blossom, send forth shoots, and fill the whole world with the fruit of knowledge of the one true God."

"And with You, the fruit is found," she responded.

Jesus reached high into the tree and then told Zoe, "Hold out your hands."

She reached out her cupped hands to Him.

With that, He began to drop many colored stones from His hands into hers, and her hands were filled to overflowing. "Be fruitful, Zoe, and multiply as these stones are multiplying before you."

She began to laugh at the abundance in her hands, and suddenly she was again in her humble little home. She looked down into her palm, and one very colorful stone remained.

"I will abide and be fruitful," she said, smiling up toward the heavens. "I will hold out Your life, this fruit You have given to me to nourish others."

She pulled out her little black pouch and added the fruit stone to the others.

She knew that He was smiling back at her.

❧ DEVOTIONAL GUIDE 64 ❧

"Jesus, in my journey to wholeness not only do I want to be changed into Your image, but I also want the knowledge of the one true God to be displayed as I live life. I know I received salvation when I received You as my Savior, but what does it mean to 'work out my salvation' when I know it is freely given by grace? Help me understand."

Jesus smiled a knowing, loving smile as He said," So many of My Body have trouble with this one. I have written down in Philippians 2:12 *'work out your own salvation with fear and trembling.'* It is easy to feel you must earn or perform to receive My life or to earn My love and favor. Not so! Grace means you are freely given based on My provision on the cross, My favor, My resurrection power, and My character simply by receiving it and walking therein. My grace has provided everything you need to fulfill My plan for your life. You simply have to unpack it and receive it the way the tree branch receives My rain, sunshine, and nutrients from the earth. As you walk in intimacy with Me, believing what I say and receiving My provision, grace happens.

"My life is the example of how you are to live. What can you learn from how I lived in order to live your life, My beloved Bride?"

"Jesus, Your Word says You never did anything You didn't see Your Father doing or saying. Is that how I am to live?"

"Yes, My beloved Bride, you are getting it. As I walked with My Father, so are you to walk with Me. This is your job of working out your salvation. In that way, as each of My Body does the same, you will do even greater things than I did because I have gone to My Father. Isn't that amazing?

"Now, one word of caution, I give to you, My beloved Bride. Just because I have said you can do all things in Me doesn't mean you are to do all things. Some think because something is needful, they must do it. Not so! I have set aside grace for what I have assigned you to do. Should there not be the grace to do a certain activity, check with Me to be sure it is your assignment. Do not presume. Presumption is not good! It is like taking over My work your way. Live as I lived in intimacy with Father. Maintain your intimacy with Me by listening and obeying My voice."

"Yes, Jesus, this helps so much. May the orchards of my garden produce rich fruit not only for me but Your Kingdom. Multiplication is my goal."

(Meditate upon the following Scriptures, asking the Holy Spirit to show you what you need to see now: John 5:19; 14:12; Philippians 2:12-16; 4:13; Psalm 19:13; and Ephesians 4:7. Write down and ponder your insights.)

My Garden Within

Devotional Guide Inventory Chapter 14

1. What is one result of sin the enemy uses to blind you to Jesus' love, mercy, and godly character? What manifestation of pain do you wrestle with the most? What is the only effective way to process pain?

2. Who alone is able to break the power of sin? What happens when you make a vow to do right in your own strength? How are the destructive generational patterns broken for you and your children?

3. Have you confused an earthly authority's harshness or abuse with your heavenly Father's heart? What is the purpose of pruning? If you are being trained or disciplined, what does that say about your relationship with God? What is to be the end result of correction by your God? What is to be the focus of the eyes of your heart?

4. What does it mean to "work out your salvation"? How did Jesus model living the Christian life? How do you live the Christian life? How do you know if a good thing that needs to be done is your assignment? How does presumption get you in trouble?

My Garden Within Inventory

CHAPTER 15

Crossing the Jordan

Truly the Lord has given all the land into our hands (Joshua 2:24).

Zoe rose early the next morning to the words, "Follow Me."

"Where are You?" she responded. Again she found herself before the River of Life in her garden. She looked across the river to notice Jesus standing on the other side.

"Follow Me," He again proclaimed.

"But how do I get over to You?" she asked as she looked to her left and to her right. She did not see any place where the river would allow her to cross, as it was moving rapidly and flowing over its banks.

Jesus shouted from the other side this proclamation: "This day I will begin to magnify Myself in you in the sight of all, so they may know that I am with you as I was with so many before."

He stepped a bit closer to the river. "You will know, Zoe, that the living God is with you wherever you go. You will also have a keen awareness of Me, because I will go before you and you will know it."

He stepped into the river and said, "Come over to this land."

At that, the river, which was just overflowing its banks, stood still far off upstream, and the ground before her became instantly dry. She stood still herself, astonished.

Again He spoke, saying, "Come into your promise."

And Zoe stepped by faith into the dry riverbed and advanced, not only to her Jesus, but also to her purpose in life. After she stepped out of the bed, her Beloved lifted her up in the air, turned, and set her into His land. With that, the waters of the river returned to their place and flowed over its banks as before.

"Remember when I first showed you this river, Zoe?"

"Yes," she said, nodding.

"Remember that in this life-giving river was the promise and that as you crossed through it you would receive everything you needed for life and godliness?"

"I do," she responded.

With confidence in His voice, He spoke. "Today it has been fulfilled. I have given you everything today that you need for the rest of your journey on this earth and in your world. It's in the crossing that you have received. Today you will know that My hand has shaped and restored your life completely."

Zoe looked down, and her attire had changed from jeans and T-shirt to a beautiful, white wedding gown. She remembered the words He had spoken to her that first time at the river: "Forever, your life and My life in you will cause others to want Me and worship Me."

DEVOTIONAL GUIDE 65

"Jesus, just as You captured Zoe's heart, You have captured mine. She heard You calling, but couldn't see how to come to You. So many times I likewise have followed You, but felt trapped somewhere I didn't expect to be and felt You tricked me or backed me into a holy corner with no way out. Help me understand how to think about this from Your perspective."

"My beloved Bride, I am excited to talk about your feelings," Jesus said with a tender smile. "Many of My loved ones have felt the same way.

Actually, My prophet Jeremiah said to Me, *'O Lord, You have persuaded and deceived me, and I was persuaded and deceived; You are stronger than I and have prevailed...'* as recorded in Jeremiah 20:7. See My beloved, you are in good company with My prophet, Jeremiah. Because My ways are so different, some of My loved ones have affectionately and reverently called Me, Jehovah Sneaky. I know their hearts that they trust My loving, sovereign hand working in their lives, and we laugh and rejoice together."

"Thanks, Jesus. I don't feel quite so badly about my feelings now...but how do I proceed?"

Jesus continued with such compassion saying, "My beloved, the Israelites, My chosen people, were landless for nearly five hundred years. Then there was a long period of slavery in Egypt. I miraculously delivered them into freedom led by Moses with forty years of testing. I trained them for living as free people under My guidance and blessing. However, they refused to believe Me when backed into a 'holy corner.' Instead, their unbelief and disobedience consumed them. Of those delivered from slavery, only Caleb and Joshua entered the Promised Land.

"Joshua and Caleb entered into My provision which is called the Promised Land because they lived from My perspective—seeing as I see. They entered My rest prepared for them. You, My beloved, can also enter My rest prepared for you today, moving forward enjoying your Promised Land with Me. I give instructions in Hebrews 4:11 as to your part: *'Let us therefore be zealous and exert ourselves and strive diligently to enter into that rest [of God, to know and experience it for ourselves]....'*

"Your job, My beloved, is to stay in My presence, listening to My voice and obeying Me as I give directions for taking your Promised Land. It is a 'holy war' for you just as it was for the Israelites. They were given the strategy of removing all evil from their land. So, as you and I walk together, we will do the same. Are you ready?"

"Yes, my Lord and Bridegroom, I am ready to allow You to guide me, direct me and lead me into Your ways of righteousness. I thank You and love You so much."

(Prayerfully and carefully read Psalm 95, Hebrews 3-4, and Jeremiah 20:7. Ask the Holy Spirit to speak to your heart giving you your next steps forward with Him. Write down your thoughts and decisions.)

My Garden Within

_____

_____

_____

She looked down into the river, and she saw the beautiful gown and the glow on her face reflecting back at her. "I am whole," she proclaimed. "You have remade me with Your love." She paused. "You have transformed me to look like You."

She knew her physical form looked nothing like Him, yet her spirit was renewed inside of her.

Jesus held out His hand to her, and in it was her little black pouch of memorial stones that she had collected from Him on her journey.

"To you, these stones shall forever be a reminder that you are made with a purpose that only you and I together can fulfill."

She received the pouch from His hand but kept unbroken eye contact with Him.

"This is the Promised Land. This journey has been about restoration, breakthrough, and crossing over into all that We have promised you and planned for you to do for Us. All of Our promises are fulfilled here in this garden. With Us, here in you, you truly live."

The more the words flowed from His mouth, the more the beauty around her grew. She believed, she really believed, that His life was now her life.

"Guard the truth in you now." He caught her attention, because she realized she still had a part to play in this flourishing life.

"Stop allowing yourself to be agitated by others, and stay in the Spirit.

Remain in Me. Keep your mind here. When it starts to stray or think negatively or complain, bring it back here to this land. There is life here. You need to live as if you are free, because you are."

She again realized her great need of His continued wisdom and revelation, even on this side of the river, and asked, "How do I stop being agitated?" She knew this was one of her greatest adversaries.

"The Holy Spirit will remind you of all you have learned here so that you can live in this flourishing state of your garden all the time."

She continued to watch life flourish around her.

"That's why I gave you the memorial stones. Get them back out and spend time with Me in the secret place, for I will strengthen you there. Meditate on Me, for I am the only One who can keep you in that undisturbed place."

She felt great peace flood her soul as she listened with her whole heart.

 # DEVOTIONAL GUIDE 66

"Jesus, since the Promised Land still has 'holy wars' in which to engage, please give me the strategy that wins these wars and keeps me in Your rest enjoying Your peace."

Jesus' joy was overflowing because He knew His beloved really meant what she was saying and would cooperate with His heart. With gentleness but firmness He began, "My beloved Bride, My instructions are laid out in Second Corinthians 10:1-6. I explain this battle is not fought with weapons according to the flesh, but there are powerful God-tools, mighty before God to smash all barriers against the truth of God. Your part is obedience and following My leading to bring you and others who you are influencing into maturity.

"There are basically three parts I want to point out to you now. First, this 'holy war' is won with weapons of My Spirit. This means you are to continue to walk in My presence not allowing anyone to draw you out but relying and trusting in Me. There and only there is the power of your foe defeated.

"Next, you are to be careful to rest in My finished work for you on the cross. You will be fitting every loose thought, emotion, and impulse into the structure of My life. You will not live from your carnal heart but from the new heart I gave you. Judge yourself to see which heart is controlling you. Are love and the fruit of My Spirit flowing as described in First Corinthians 13:4-8 and Galatians 5:22-23—kindness, patience, not being provoked, peace, longsuffering, self-control, and the like? The opposite fruit from the carnal flesh is hatred, jealousies, uncleanness, lustful pleasure, and outburst of wrath, disunity, strife, and the like. When the flesh is manifest, quickly turn back to Me allowing My heart to flow through your new heart I gave you remaining in My presence.

"My beloved, as you follow Me in this way, you are allowing no disobedience within yourself. Likewise, you do not condone or support another's carnal flesh or their disobedience as we have discussed earlier.

"Last, remember this is a 'holy war' in which only My Spirit can cast down arguments and every high thing that exalts itself against the knowledge of God. Keep your eyes upon Me, your heart in My hand, and watch My victory be accomplished. Are you willing to walk this way with Me to possess your Promised Land?"

"Yes, Jesus, I am. I trust You to direct my thoughts, regulate my emotions, and direct my will for Your glory to be released. I am comforted knowing You are holding me in Your righteous right hand."

(Meditate upon the following Scriptures, asking the Holy Spirit to open the eyes of your heart to see what is needful for your next steps: 2 Corinthians 10:1-6; 1 Corinthians 11:31; 13:4-8; Galatians 5:19-24. Write down what speaks to you. Review until you have fully embraced all you see.)

 My Garden Within

_____

_____

_____

"And when you are teaching others, teach them to go all the way into the Promised Land, not just halfway. Tell them not to settle for half the promise. In other words, tell them they must not settle for half the weeds remaining in their gardens, saying of themselves, 'Oh well, the rest of my garden looks okay.' No, convince them that the weeds remaining will multiply and try to take over their whole garden life."

She thought about a verse she had recently read in her Bible about Abraham, who was at the time called Abram because God had not yet given him his new name. It said of him that on the way to the Promised Land he came to Haran and settled there.

Zoe asked Jesus, "Haran was halfway to the Promised Land, wasn't it?"

He loved the wisdom that continued growing in her.

"Yes, it was. Circumstances, situations, the enemy, and even your own thoughts always try to talk you out of what God has said and done in you. Just like in the Garden of Eden at the beginning of the Bible, where the serpent came into the Garden and said, 'Did God really say not to eat the fruit of this tree? ' or maybe now asks, 'Do you really think you are healed of your past?' He'll even say things like 'You are not good enough' or 'Every time you open your mouth you sound stupid' or 'You need to do this or that first, before you can ever do anything for God, before you can hand someone some of your fruit.' The enemy will always lie to you, because that is who he is."

Zoe felt His fruitfulness filling her soul.

Jesus continued, "Don't just go halfway into the fullness and fruitfulness God has for your soul. Cross all the way into the things that I have promised you. Tell others what took place in you today, and then tell them to cross their Jordan and to go into their Promised Land. You need to hold on to the promises I have given to you and tell others to cling to their promises also."

She thought about all the half-truths she had once believed about herself.

"The whole world, including a lot of Christians, is stuck, Zoe. People are stuck halfway into the Promised Land. Convince them to cross over like you have today and then to give out the life and the fruit that they have received. That's also what I desire from you, Zoe—to give what you have been given by spending intimate time with Me, your Maker. Then the ones you touch can become a flourishing garden too, able to hand out life-giving fruit, which is nourishment to others."

Zoe smiled widely and said, "You have given me the key to this life of nourishing others; I now know it to be intimacy with You. Time spent with You is the key to this flourishing garden life."

DEVOTIONAL GUIDE 67

"Jesus, as I am enjoying being with You, I often see someone who appears to be so much more mature or gifted than I am and I lose hope and perspective. I get in their presence rather than Yours. How can this be corrected?"

Jesus' smile was unusually wide and joyful as He said, "I love your questions and your reasoning. You know I made you that way, don't you? Continue to be yourself. I love and delight to be with you.

"Your question is solved as you learn to live with Me where you are seated with Me in the heavenly realm. After I secured your salvation on the cross, I picked you up and set you down with Me in the highest heaven with Me at the right hand of My Father. Imagine this truth, My beloved. Remember, you are in Me. It is a matter of learning to see with the eyes of your heart what is really true as explained in My Word written down for you. It is learning to live in two worlds at the same time. Your feet are firmly planted on earth walking out your purpose here, but the real you is seated with Me in the heavenly realm. As you dwell upon this perspective you not only live in the Kingdom of God now, but you also bring the Kingdom of heaven to earth for others.

"When you are tempted to walk in another person's presence or be intimated by their gifts, maturities, or blessings, use this tool to redirect your focus back to Me. Let's adjust slightly a tool firefighters use to enable people to put a fire out when clothes are inflamed. They say, 'Stop, drop, and roll.' Let's apply this to focusing back on Me where you are seated with Me. 'Stop' being entangled with comparing yourself with others, 'drop' into Me by refocusing on Me not others, and 'roll' all of your cares on Me, and I would add 'Be quiet' in Me until your focus is back where we are seated in heavenly places far above the enemy's reach. I love the other person just as I love you. Each has his or her place in My Kingdom. We are not in competition, but are to be completing each other. I am putting My Body together and I need your help. Love the other person and love yourself. We are family—next of kin. What you do to them, you do to Me.

"Learn to live your life before an audience of One—Me. When you awake in the morning, do everything to please Me, for Me, and with Me, allowing us to enjoy being together. If someone comes to your home, you have already prepared it for Me and they simply join us. If no one comes, you and I have a delightful time. Such a lifestyle eliminates the scurrying around to get ready for company. You are already entertaining Me. I am seated in deep heaven, in charge of running the universe, galaxies, and governments. I am the One who has the final say, and you and I can enjoy each other's company as a way of life. This is living, My beloved. You are doing each and everything as unto Me. This lifestyle will eliminate your comparison with others and your attachment to the world that is unhealthy. Does this make sense, My beloved?"

"Yes, it does, my Beloved Jesus. With Your help, I will live supernaturally in two worlds at the same time, thereby bringing forth Your Kingdom within and around me as a way of life. I love loving You. I want to love You as much as You love me."

(Ponder carefully the following Scriptures: Ephesians 2:6; Colossians 3:1-4; 1 Peter 5:7; 2 Corinthians 10:12; and 1 Corinthians 10:31. Write down what you want to embrace for the next step in your journey to wholeness. Review it regularly.)

My Garden Within

_____

_____

_____

Jesus smiled in return and replied, "In the garden things are constant. I am constant in every circumstance. Most people respond in the flesh to the situations and circumstances surrounding them. I want you to respond in the Spirit, with Me holding your every thought and action. Let's see. Let Me give you an example."

Zoe loved the way He always knew how to word things so that she would grasp the truth He was revealing.

"It is like the difference between a thermometer and a thermostat. Thermometers go up and down depending on the weather—or the situation, in this instance. That is like the flesh, which says 'I'm up' or 'I'm down' and is always changing. But a thermostat is different: you set it and it stays there, and it has the ability to change a room's temperature. That is walking in My Spirit—setting your mind on Me constantly and responding with Me in your thoughts and actions. So when you walk into a room or a situation, conscious of Me walking with and in you, that alone has the ability to change the atmosphere of that room or situation."

Zoe loved that even in the Promised Land He continued to teach her. She loved to be taught by the Lord.

"So, Zoe, when your flesh starts to rule and you feel it changing the temperature of peace, encourage yourself in the Lord your God. Speak to your soul, tell it to be quiet, and set your every thought on Me. Take a peace break. Walk away from the situation for a moment, and focus on My plan for it. I always have a plan." He grinned. "Come to the garden, remind Me of My promises, and remind yourself what I have said to you. And when discouragement and depression start, right then pray. Talk to Me, and then listen. Let My peace rule as an umpire in your heart continuously."

Zoe visualized her Jesus in a baseball umpire suit and giggled.

He said, "Yep, that's My job." He made the "safe" gesture, as an umpire would make with a runner sliding into a base. "I call you safe," He said.

And she felt safe in Him.

~~ DEVOTIONAL GUIDE 68 ~~

"Jesus, I want Your peace to rule as umpire for me as a way of life. I think this is called living on the narrow road that few find. I don't want to settle for a halfway or a comfortable place. I want Your balanced life in the Spirit, not my tendency to write people off or try too hard to fix them or myself. I want to cooperate with You bringing forth the good and refusing the vile. Please give insight into Your narrow way, Jesus."

Jesus said with much love and tender delight, "My beloved Bride your statement fills My heart full of joy. The narrow road is obedience to Me with the confidence I have done well by you, combined with your commitment to suffer well with Me. When you live in My presence doing what I know to be best for you, you are building a life which is absolutely indestructible, 'on the Rock,' which is Me. Nothing can shake you. You become secure and stable resting in My peace, which only I can give. By living this way, you are being My disciple.

"Your suffering well with Me means realizing any pain you push through is cooperating with Me to bring forth My image in you, thereby becoming the person I created you to be before the foundation of the world. The suffering you go through on behalf of others, who are struggling to yield to Me, is also for the same purpose. This is the way we bring to harvest the fruit I want in your life and the life of others. It is hard work. You must work at not taking personally what happens, but seeking My heart for you and others. See that your heart is free from hatred and unforgiveness. Even though it is hard, it is worth it because it is the only way to truly live the abundant life.

"You, My beloved Bride, are learning to not only reign with Me now suffering through your own pain, but you are also cooperating with Me in helping to finish the remainder of My sufferings for My Body, the Church. I paid for sin on the cross, but being formed into My image is painful. You help when you bear with them for Me. We all win—you, them, and Me. When you love your enemies, they taste of Me, and you are stretched to love when it doesn't come easy. You look more like Me. They have an opportunity to come to Me through the window of light you shine forth. You have joined Me in suffering on their behalf and being a vessel to show them My life.

"Know we are doing this together. I am strengthening you from within as well as interceding for you and them as you move forward. You are learning to reign with Me now, which will also have eternal benefits. Isn't that good news?"

"Yes, my Beloved Bridegroom, that is very good news. Now I have a better perspective and reason for embracing what has been so hard before. I choose the narrow road with You."

(Carefully and prayerfully meditate on the following Scriptures, asking the Holy Spirit to give you the wisdom and revelation needed for your next steps: Matthew 7:14; 20:16; 1 Corinthians 10:4; Romans 8:23,26,34; Colossians 1:24; 3:15; 2 Timothy 2:12-13; and Revelation 22:5. Write down what is meaningful to you and bask in it until it is yours.)

My Garden Within

_____

_____

_____

He said, "The enemy sometimes makes halfway feel comfortable. It's like when you get used to the cold if you've been in it for awhile. He does this to keep you from going all the way into fullness and fruitfulness, and he will make you comfortable where you are." He placed one hand on His chest and His other on hers. "Enter all the way into all that I have promised and said of you. Believe and cling to them and to Me. You have the ability to change the world, because I am walking in it with you."

Zoe hated the cold; she had no desire to stay there physically or spiritually.

"Stay completely within the fullness of what I have for you; it's in the crossing that you give out the abundant life. Work with and for Me, and give what you've been given. Plant in others and water others, and I will make them grow."

As He said this, all of a sudden something appeared before them that looked like a scroll, and as it rolled open they were looking at the earth from a different place.

Could this be the view from heaven? she wondered. She could see the earth revolving and was astounded by the scene before her.

"The whole earth is groaning, wanting the children of the living God to arise." He placed His hand on the side of her head, and they were face to face. "Arise now, Zoe, My life giver, and shine. Pour forth and give life to those I have appointed you to; give My life. They are waiting. Some may not know it yet, but they are waiting."

He reassured her with a smile. "My words are nourishment, and people could die without the nourishment or truth that you have in you. I have qualified you to tell others of My goodness and to make My life available to them. Teach, admonish, and train. I need you. Others need you, and you need others. Encourage one another in Me."

He looked out into the sky and seemed to make a star shine brighter just with a glance. "In teaching you will learn, and in learning you will teach."

Zoe was so captivated, not only by Him, but also by the view before her eyes. "The universe declares Your glory," she said with a quiver in her voice as she continued to gaze down at the world and across the universe.

"I just want you to know something," He said.

Her gaze returned to Him.

"There is no responsibility on you for this work; the only responsibility you have is to keep in living, constant touch with Me and to not allow anything at all to hinder your cooperation with Me."

DEVOTIONAL GUIDE 69

"Jesus, Your last words to Your disciples were to go and make disciples of all the nations. Are those words equally for me and others? If so, will You help me understand what this means?"

Jesus wrapped me in His loving warm smile as He said, "Yes, My beloved Bride, this does apply to you. You are to first of all become My disciple, which is what you have been doing. When you accepted Me as your Savior, you began your Christian journey. However, when you gave yourself to Me without restraint in abandonment to love Me with all your mind, soul, and heart, walking with Me intimately as a way of life, your discipleship began. Being a disciple means walking with Me and learning to live as I would live your life if I were you. In this process you fall in love with Me. You begin enjoying being yourself as I created you to be and spreading My light and life in whatever career or setting I lead you to live. You, in turn, lead and teach others the truth you grasp and are learning. Each truth you embrace and each victory gained in your life gives you authority to release the same to others. You love them as yourself. That is being a disciple and making disciples.

"Just as I sent My disciples out with the words, 'Lo, I am sending you out as sheep in the midst of wolves; be wary and wise as serpents, and be innocent—harmless, guileless and without falsity—as doves,' I give you the same instructions. A snake is watchful and observant until the time is right to act. One rarely sees a snake chasing its prey or thrashing about in an effort to impress it. When it acts, it acts quickly and decisively. A dove has single vision. Likewise, your eyes are to be singularly on Me. A dove is incapable of intrigue, guile, or misleading behavior. Your needed traits are in turn founded in patience, confidence, hopefulness, truthfulness, and genuine respect for the freedom and individuality of others, which the dove has.

"My disciples will reflect the same attitude as Paul when he said he had learned to be content in whatever circumstance he found himself, whether it was with plenty or little. By contentment I mean being satisfied to the point where you are not disturbed or disquieted regardless of what is going on. This is a process, but it is to continue being your direction and goal."

"Jesus, I love being Your disciple and making disciples with You. When I am being a holy bridge for You to Your disciples bearing their burdens with them, will You show me how and when to release them to carry their own load?"

"Be encouraged, My beloved Bride. I am faithful to do in you what I have called you to do. Each situation is different and I cannot give you a formula or specific steps. However, as you seek Me, the Holy Spirit will lead you. You have worked hard and I know your heart. You will continue to stay in My presence and allow Me to prepare you for receiving My words written down in Matthew 25:34: *'Come, you blessed of My Father…inherit…the kingdom prepared for you from the foundation of the world.'*"

"Jesus, just as Your original disciples turned the world upside down for You, I want to do the same. I yield myself to You, knowing You will finish in Me what you have begun. Thank You!"

(Ponder the following Scriptures, writing down what the Holy Spirit shows you: Matthew 28:19; 10:16; 25:34; Philippians 4:10-13; 1:6; Galatians 6:2, 5; and 1 Thessalonians 5:24. Write down the thoughts coming to you. Review them until you are sure what your next step is.)

My Garden Within

His voice was filled with more compassion than she had ever heard in Him as He spoke directly into her soul.

"The things that used to keep your life pinned down are gone. They are gone, Zoe."

Tears once again flowed from her eyes.

"You are free for one purpose only—to be absolutely devoted to Me and to share Me with those around you. Take hold of My strength, the strength that I provide, and completely surrender to My protection. I pray that My roots will go down deep inside you and that you will blossom, send forth shoots, and fill the whole world with the knowledge of the one true God…of Me."

Zoe looked back to the earth, and they were instantly back in her garden, back to the first place where she entered into her soul with Jesus by her side. The garden that had once looked so dead was now filled with life, blossoms, color, and vibrancy. She hardly recognized the place and could not believe the change.

She was standing on the path where she first saw the signs of life inside her and said, "You know, Jesus, when we first came here, this path was covered with thistles and thorns, but just look what You have done! You have caused my garden to flourish and to be fruitful." She continued looking around, and then she looked back at Him. "I love to be here with You, and I will come here every day. You made it alive again; you made me live again."

She took in a deep breath. So thankful. So alive.

DEVOTIONAL GUIDE 70

"You have drawn me with cords of Your love, my Beloved Bridegroom. I am held in Your embrace knowing 'My beloved is mine, and I am His! Your desire is toward me!' I can rest, allowing You to do what brings You glory because 'I trust in You, O Lord; saying, 'You are my God; my times are in Your hand; You are my chosen and assigned portion, my cup.' Your Word comforts me, Jesus."

Jesus' voice was filled with more compassion than I have ever heard when He spoke directly into my soul saying, "My beautiful Bride, let us rejoice! As you have walked with Me, obeyed My voice and allowed Me to be your all in all, you are preparing yourself for the marriage of the Lamb, which is Me. Celebrate the days ahead with Me. I have shown you what is good and what I require of you—to do justly and to love kindness and mercy, and to humble yourself and walk humbly with Me. I will help you to remember My work is accomplished not by might, nor by power, but by My Spirit."

"My Beloved Bridegroom, I desire to hasten Your coming by living in Your presence with my heart in Your hand. I, Your Bride and the Spirit say, 'Come!' Let all who hear say, 'Come!' Let all who thirst, come. Whoever desires let them take the water of life freely."

(With a heart open to Jesus, ask the Holy Spirit to bring life into you as you meditate upon the following Scriptures: Song of Solomon 2:16; 7:10; Psalm 31:14-15; Micah 6:8; Zechariah 4:6; 2 Peter 3:12; and Revelation 22:17. Write down your revelation and bask in it.)

Please visit Appendix D to build up your spirit as you overcome abuse—whether sexual, physical, or emotional—as given by Arthur Burk. Be patient with yourself during your journey. Jesus is! Remember, it's a lifetime journey!

My Garden Within

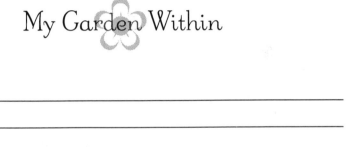

_____

_____

_____

Devotional Guide Inventory Chapter 15

1. Have you ever felt "tricked" or backed into a "holy corner" by Jesus? What did Jeremiah feel? What kept the Israelites out of their Promised Land? Which of their weaknesses do you struggle with the most? How are you discovering to enter into His rest for yourself?

2. Are you aware of "holy wars" going on about you? What is the weapon by which holy wars are won? What is your part in cooperating with God's Spirit? Which area is the hardest for you to have victory over at this time? Who casts down the barriers and strongholds set up against the Lord?

3. Do you struggle with getting in others' presence thereby becoming discouraged or intimidated? Have you ever grasped the truth you are seated with Jesus in heaven right now? Are you realizing you are to live in two realms at the same time—your feet on earth and your heart in heaven? How does this feel to you? How are you learning to "Stop, drop, roll" and "Be quiet"? How are you to see yourself as completing the Body of Christ by loving others rather than being in competition with them? How does living before an audience of One simplify your life?

4. What is the narrow road? What are the benefits of walking on the narrow road? What does suffering well mean? What is the hardest part of suffering well for you? How do we help finish the suffering left to be completed on behalf of Jesus' Body? What does this mean and not mean? Who are you in partnership with for this process?

5. Are you to be making disciples? What is a disciple? How do you gain authority in your life? What does being as wise as a serpent mean? What does it mean to be as gentle as a dove? Are you content? If not, why? How do you know when to be a bridge for bearing others' burdens on Jesus' behalf and when to release them to carry their own load?

6. Do you feel the cords of His love drawing you? Do you know He's yours and that His desire is for you? Do you trust Him to regulate your schedule? Is He your portion? What are your general instructions for living your days ahead with your Bridegroom, Jesus?

Now read the conclusion of Zoe's journey.

Jesus smiled and placed Zoe's last stone, a round one, in her palm.

"It looks like the earth," she said, and she smiled.

"When you find Me in your heart, you will find Me everywhere. Your garden is alive now. It's alive and awake. And if you look outside of it and gaze with My eyes, you will see that the whole world is a garden."

At that last statement, Zoe was standing in her physical garden at home. She looked out into her world and smiled.

The end—or, actually, just the beginning.

But thanks be to God, Who in Christ always leads us in triumph [as trophies of Christ's victory] and through us spreads and makes evident the fragrance of the knowledge of God everywhere (2 Corinthians 2:14).

Behold the days are coming, says the Lord...that everything heretofore barren and unfruitful shall overflow with spiritual blessing (Amos 9:13).

...Indeed, in the whole world [that Gospel] is bearing fruit and still is growing... (Colossians 1:6).

The gardens around me are blooming now.

Zoe

My Garden Within Inventory

APPENDIX A

Deliverance from Evil Entities

The following suggested prayers are simply guidelines. Please allow the Holy Spirit to make adjustments according to each individual situation. It is recommended that prayer counseling deliverance be done with one or two mentors who have not only experienced deliverance, but who also co-labor with like-minded Christians providing covering for successful Kingdom work.

Introduction

"To the Ancient of Days, True, Holy Creator God, in the name of the True Lord Jesus Christ I come to You. I ask You to move back all cosmic beings (all levels of evil in Satan's realm as in Ephesians 6:12) and forbid them to harass, intimidate, or retaliate against _____ or any part of him/her, whether in the body or outside the body. Will You also prevent these beings, of whatever rank, to not be allowed to send any level of spiritual evil as retaliation against me here or my family, ministry, or possessions. Lord Jesus, I ask You, in accordance with Jude 8-10, to rebuke, bring a judgment, or decree against all painful, unholy connections. I trust You, my Sovereign God, to make it safe to work here today, in the name of the True Lord Jesus Christ and Savior."

Submission Prayer

"Lord Jesus Christ, I believe that You died on the cross for my sins and rose again from the dead. You redeemed me by Your blood, and I belong to You. I thank You, Lord Jesus, for your shed blood, which cleanses me from all sin. I want to live for You. I come to You as My Deliverer."

Repent

"I now confess my sin of 'putting up with,' 'entertaining,' and for 'agreeing with' evil entities even unknowingly by catering to their demands and desires. I now repent of these areas and ask You to bring to my mind specific areas and things I have done." (You are to wait, allowing the Holy Spirit to bring to mind any areas or specific sins He wants you to confess. After this time of specifics is finished, conclude by confessing all known or unknown sins.) I repent of them and ask You to forgive me. I renounce them all."

Forgive

"I forgive others as I want You to forgive me. Holy Spirit, bring to my mind anyone involved in this area of my life that I need to forgive." (Wait. Name each one and forgive them. After this time is finished, repent of all the ways you have given place to the enemy. Forgive yourself. Ask God to forgive you now and cleanse you with Jesus' blood. Thank Jesus for cleansing you.)

Renounce

"Jesus, You know my special need: to obtain freedom from things that bind me, torment me, and defile me. I need freedom from every foreign, alien, or demonic entity. I claim the promise of Your Word, "Whoever calls upon the name of the Lord Jesus Christ shall be delivered."

Command

"I call upon You now, Lord Jesus, to deliver me and set me free. I renounce Satan, all his works, all his workers, and all uncleanness. I renounce, break, and loose myself from all evil, unclean spirits in the name of Jesus Christ. I ask you, angels of God, to enforce this command now on any foreign, alien, or demonic entity present and to bring about compliance. Using the authority given to me by Jesus, you must go be the footstool of Jesus as Psalm 110:1 says. All this I do in the name, and on the authority, of Jesus Christ of Nazareth. Thank You Lord Jesus. Amen!"

Restore

Pray for a new infilling of the Holy Spirit into all of the newly cleared out regions within you. Pray for physical, soul, and spirit healing of any damage done by the presence of the unclean entities. Pray the Holy Spirit will make you very sensitive and aware of falling back into old thought patterns or sinful habits that would begin to reopen any doors.

APPENDIX B

Breaking Ungodly Soul Ties

Ungodly soul ties are invisible ties, agreements, covenants that bind to another person, organization, or things. Ungodly soul ties create emotional and spiritual connections with another person that are perverted, dysfunctional, and/or sexual. This causes a form of co-dependency between the ones making the wrong agreements. God "honors," or recognizes, these covenants. He leaves each one of us free to decide when and if we will appropriate His provisions to break or cut the ties and release ourselves from the attachment from a person, organization, or thing. The other person is also set free in the process. Ungodly soul ties could be compared to having a number of rubber bands attached to your head by each person with whom you have had an unhealthy, emotional, or sexual relationship. The rubber bands exert pressure that pulls you toward each of these people. As you try to move forward in life, you feel pulled in many directions. You don't feel free, and you are not free. These soul ties need to be broken.

Introduction

"Father, in the name of Jesus Christ of Nazareth, I submit to You. I submit my soul, my desires, and my emotions to You."

Repent

Repent of any sins that involve that person whether it is adultery, fornication, or expecting a need to be met by this person that only Jesus can meet.

Forgive

Forgive the person of any wrongs done. Forgive yourself for your part of the involvement. Forgiveness releases bitterness and releases both you and the other person. State you will no longer be angry at yourself, hate yourself, or punish yourself. The same is true for your thoughts toward the other person.

Renounce

If you have made any spoken communication, vows or even simply said to a former lover, etc., "I will love you forever," it has ample power in the spiritual realm to bind you to another person in ungodly soul ties. The tongue is quite capable of binding the soul and can be a significant means to create soul ties: *"You are snared by the words of your mouth; you are taken by the words of your mouth"* (Proverbs 6:2 NKJV). These spoken covenants need to be renounced in order to break the soul tie. You have said it verbally—break it verbally.

"Father, in Jesus' name, I loose myself from all relationships that are not ordained of God. I loose myself from all relationships that are not of the Spirit but of the flesh. I loose myself from all relationships based on control, domination, or manipulation. All relationships based on lust and deception. I repent for my part of control, domination, or manipulation to _____ and forgive _____ for his/her part in such activities.

"Lord, I break my soul/psychic ties with _____. I release myself from him/her, and I release him/her from me. As I do this, Lord, I pray You will cause him/her to be all You want him/her to be, and that You would cause me to be all that You want me to be.

"Lord, please cleanse my mind from all memories of ungodly unions, so I am totally free to give myself to You and to others in a godly way.

"I ask You to charge your angels to go and retrieve the fragmented pieces of my soul and return them to their original position. I renounce and cancel the assignments of all evil spirits attempting to maintain these ungodly soul ties or that may have been transferred to me through association."

Restore

"Father, I receive Your forgiveness for all past sex/soulish/psychic sins. I believe I am totally forgiven. Thank You for remembering my sins no more. Thank You for restoring my soul to wholeness. Thank You for cleansing me from all unrighteousness. I choose to walk in holiness by Your grace. I commit myself totally to You. Please keep me holy in my spirit, soul, and body. I praise You, in Jesus' name. Amen."

Return or Destroy

Gifts also symbolize a relationship and can hold a soul tie in place. If you have a ring, personal gifts, cards, jewelry, or other "relationship gifts" from a previous relationship, it is time to get rid of them.

Flee

Not only are you to withdraw from all ungodly aspects of these relationships, but you are also to flee any area of temptation while submitting to God, standing firm against the devil, which causes him to flee. See Second Timothy 2:22 and James 4:7.

APPENDIX C

Breaking Ungodly Generational Inheritances

The effects of gross or deeply established patterns of sin in a person can be passed from one generation to another according to Exodus 34:7: *"He will by no means leave the guilty unpunished, visiting the iniquity of fathers on the children and on the grandchildren to the third and fourth generations"* (New American Standard Bible). This was seen in the lives of the Israelites. Their failure to live up to God's standards of righteousness resulted in many generations suffering from a host of curses released upon them (Deuteronomy 11:26-28). These inherited consequences of sin can actually be carried through an ancestral line for many more generations than three or four because every time a new generation engages in the sin, the inheritance gets extended another three or four generations (Lamentations 5:1-18).

What seems to occur in generational inheritances is that subsequent generations experience an increased temptation to succumb to the same sin(s) of their ancestors. The accumulated guilt and curses connected to that sin may not be released upon a particular person, however, until the person actually engages in the sin (Matthew 23:34-35).

Confession overcomes personal and generational sin in someone's life (Psalm 106, Jeremiah 3:22–4:2, and Daniel 9:3-19). This will not only remove the heightened tendency to sin in the way of the person's ancestors and the curses that come from doing so, but it will also break the chain of inheritance from flowing any further to succeeding generations. It may even open the way for blessing to flow into the generational line instead (Exodus 5-6).

Introduction

"Father, in the name of Jesus Christ of Nazareth, the Anointed One, I come to You today asking the Holy Spirit to direct my prayer, allowing You to accomplish all that is on Your heart today for me and my generations."

Repent/Forgiveness

"Lord, I confess that my ancestors sinned both knowingly and unknowingly and opened doors of ungodly generation pattern and contamination into my life. I acknowledge, confess, and renounce my parents', grandparents', and previous generations' sinful acts of _____." Be specific about one area of sin at a time.

"Lord, I confess I carried the sins on by coming into agreement with the enemy even though I didn't realize I was doing so. Now I stand in the gap and intercede for the sins of my ancestors." Express your genuine forgiveness of them for bringing the inherited iniquity of _____ and its consequences into your life. Be specific about the consequences that you have borne as a result of this inheritance or any curses you recognize in relationship to it.

"Lord, forgive me for how I also continued to sin in the same ways." Be specific. "Cleanse me and help me to choose to forgive myself and accept myself as forgiven."

Renounce/Break

"Lord in Your powerful name, I break this generational sin of _____ and its curses from my life and from the lives of my descendants through the shed blood of Jesus Christ on the Cross of Calvary. I not only renounce these sinful patterns and cycles of behavior now, I also break their power to influence my life and my generations going forward.

"Lord, remove any evil entities, whether foreign, alien, or demonic, that gained access to me because of this generational sin. Seal all portals that were used by these evil entities."

Restoration

"I receive your empowerment to live in righteousness, Lord. I press into You and speak Your Word over every area of my life. I am becoming what You want me to be. I choose to believe that my understanding of my call, purpose, and destiny is free to unfold starting now. I ask You to help me embrace Your words through Your servant, Jeremiah, '*I know the thoughts and plans that I have for you, for welfare and peace and not for evil, to give you hope in your final outcome.*' Thank You, my Father, for dreaming about me and putting into me everything I need to fulfill my destiny.

"I declare that the flood of blessings of my generations may now come into my life. I thank You, Lord, for releasing them now. Amen."

APPENDIX D

A Special Blessing

The following blessing is specifically for those molested; however, all have been abused whether sexually, physically, or emotionally to some degree or another. Put your name in the blank space and allow the Holy Spirit to minister to you as needed.

I call your spirit to connect with Father's Spirit. He has known you before the foundation of the world. He has watched you grow and be hungry to return to wholeness. You are developing character and being fearless to not run away from problems. Father is excited about giving you additional tools, as the spirit, to address this issue.

Ministering to the Spirit Regarding Molestation

by Arthur Burk

Speak to your human spirit; spirit, let's go back to the beginning, to the foundation. Spirit, I want to reiterate the fact that God designed you from His very nature. You are a composite of truth and light that came from the nature of God, and God has never been violated. God has been opposed; God has had many enemies, but God's boundaries are secure. God does not carry in His being a generational memory of violation.

So, spirit, as you were designed by God, you were designed with what one song writer described as a child who has never known pain. You came into the world with the ability to explosively celebrate. You came into this world with the pain-free existence of a spirit that God has designed with His complete lack of fear, His complete lack of shame, His complete lack of being intimidated. God does not sit around and worry about what the devil may do next. There's an awareness of His enemy, but there's no defensiveness on the part of God. And, spirit, that is what you carry from before conception. And that is what you are capable of returning to being, so that there is no residue; there is no cautiousness; there is no nervous tic in your soul or spirit as different stimuli cause you to put the guard up. You are capable of becoming once again that unfettered, free spirit full of joy and anticipation, engaging life without those burrs.

Now, spirit, what happened to you was incredibly defiling. The physical act of violating somebody's sexual boundaries defiles the spirit. I don't know if anyone has even acknowledged that to you before, but I want to say that very clearly. Sex is a spiritual issue. When your boundaries were violated physically, you, the spirit, receive defilement from the other person's spirit. I acknowledge that. I understand that the defilement was toxic and that it stained deeply.

Spirit, with your permission, I want to use Hebrews 4:12 and ask God to separate your spirit from theirs. So, Father, as _____ has clearly said yes, I invoke that verse. You have said that Your word is sharper than any double-edged sword. You are capable of separating soul from spirit. Father, I ask now that You would take that sword of Jesus Christ and that You would separate everything that is _____'s spirit from the individual or individuals who violated her [or his] boundaries, every place where her spirit was mingled with their spirit. I ask that you would disengage that mingling, that you would remove their presence, the presence of their spirit from her spirit.

I ask also that you would separate their soul from her soul that every soul tie would be severed, would be obliterated in a way that could never be connected again for toxicity to flow.

Father, I ask that you would establish a safe boundary around her spirit. It says in scripture that you have determined the boundaries for us, and the lines have fallen in pleasant places. I ask that that breach in the natural boundaries to her spirit would be repaired. I ask that Your God-given boundaries that could not be established when there was a commingling of spirits would now be reestablished, and that her only sharing of spirit would be righteous—with her spouse, with her community of faith. Reestablish the boundaries so that there is no possibility of that individual or those individuals' souls reconnecting. May they never find a familiar landing pad because You have established the boundaries in pleasant places.

Now, spirit, I want to challenge you to step up in some specific areas. First of all, you have in you every single thing you need to completely heal from this, to return to that place of joyousness, to that place that your guard does not go up when certain areas are bumped. I don't know how you're going to get there, but I know that God has already given you what you need.

So, spirit, each time somebody bumps an old memory, each time there's a color, a shape, a time, a place that irritates you, you need to swiftly turn away from that pain, turn your face to the Father and say, "Father, where's that data? Where's that truth? What is it that you've already placed in me that will enable me to respond to this rightly? It is already there. And each time you are bumped, use that as a trigger, as a reminder not to go back and come into agreement with your pain, but to go forward by asking God to unpack something new.

Your process will be unique. You've read other people's processes; you've heard other people's stories. Yours will be one of a kind. God has placed things about Him in your spirit that you will need for the healing.

Spirit, that moves you from the position of victim to the position of dominion—to the position of being able to partner with God in becoming whole. Spirit, you well know that there is a bigness about you. Spirit, you know that there is an immensity about you that does not come from your culture, does not come from your birth family that is bigger than your environment. And I say to you that you have held back on that bigness because of your culture.

Your culture has encouraged you to fit in with your community; your culture has encouraged you not to stand out. Your culture has encouraged you not to become prominent above your community. And, spirit, I don't know how God is going to solve that problem because He placed you in your culture, and He made you bigger than most of the people you run with. That is God's compensation to you, God's gift to you of something bigger than you.

I invite you to stop suppressing your bigness, to stop pushing down the gift that God has given to you, and, rather, to go to the Father and say, "How do we solve this mystery? How do I live with the person that I am, in the culture that you placed me in, when our culture is uncomfortable with people who rise above the norm?"

I don't have the answer for you, spirit, but I know that God didn't make a mistake. And I know God made you big. I would invite you to begin to come into agreement with God, every time you feel that stirring of greatness within you, by saying, "I know, God, that this is You. I know that I'm made to carry a huge compensation for the evil that happened to me. Now, Father, teach me how. Teach me how."

Come into agreement with your future, not your past. Come into agreement with dominion, not victimization. Come into agreement with the fact that there has to be a way, rather than with thinking I don't see a way.

Spirit, I give you permission to go to the Father as many times as you need, to go to the Father to unpack all of the treasures of the resources for healing and the power to be transformational.

And, spirit, I want to speak to one final thing, and that is revenge. God said, "Vengeance is mine saith the Lord," and the sin against you was a sin against Him. I want you to understand that the desire for vindication is godly. Nehemiah said, "God, remember what people are saying and doing to me. Take it into account." In the letter to the church of Philadelphia, God promised to vindicate people. Jesus Christ, in His high priestly prayer, said, "O.K., I'm done with this whole stable, earthly, crucifixion thing. I'm ready to be glorified. Give back to Me the glory I had when I was with You."

So understand, spirit, that God wants to avenge Himself on His enemy for what happened to you, and you have a righteous desire to be vindicated in the eyes of God and man. God will avenge Himself by making you dangerous. If God makes you whole, He has not avenged Himself. He has only healed you. God desires to avenge Himself on His ancient enemy by making you incredibly transformational, incredibly dangerous in this world, to make the enemy wish that he had never messed with you.

I bless you, as you become God's agent for Him to avenge Himself on His ancient enemy. It is right that you be hugely transformational, and there is a way for you to walk that out in your culture. I bless you, spirit, and invite you to take your place with huge legitimacy, with boldness, with freedom in our community of faith, as someone who God has chosen to be highly dangerous. I bless you, spirit, in Jesus' name.

NOTES AND SCRIPTURE REFERENCES

The Lord sat with me as I wrote this book, which came from studying the Scriptures and going through previous journals with Him. Therefore I have used *pieces or ideas* from all of the following Scriptures taken from the Amplified Bible. After reading the book, I encourage you to look up the Scripture references listed here and ask Jesus for more revelation. For more encouragement or to contact me, visit my website: www.gardenwithinministries.com. –Emma Kelln

Pieces or ideas from Scriptures were taken from the Amplified Bible. Other versions used throughout are cited on the copyright page.

CHAPTER 1: THE GARDEN

John 10:7

Song of Solomon 1:3

Psalm 119:103

Song of Solomon 4:12

Song of Solomon 2:10

Song of Solomon 1:6

Jeremiah 1:5

Hebrews 12:2

Song of Solomon 2:10

Song of Solomon 2:14

CHAPTER 2: A SECRET PROCESS

Ecclesiastes 3:1

Hosea 10:12

Genesis 50:20

Hosea 2:15

Isaiah 27:6

Song of Solomon 5:1-2

CHAPTER 3: AWAKENED

Song of Solomon 5:16

Song of Solomon 1:15

Song of Solomon 4:12

Joel 2:25

2 Kings 8:6

Song of Solomon 2:3

Song of Solomon 2:6

CHAPTER 4: DARK BUT COMELY

1. Song of Solomon 1, footnotes in Amplified Bible, pages 966-967, slightly adapted.

2. "Amazing Grace" written by John Newton.

Psalm 56:8

Ezekiel 36:35

Joshua 4

CHAPTER 5: FOUNDATION

Ephesians 4:29

Proverbs 18:21

Psalm 19:14

CHAPTER 6: PURPOSE

Jeremiah 31:3

Psalm 91:1

Song of Solomon 8:14

Song of Solomon 7:1

Song of Solomon 6:1

CHAPTER 7: LIFE

1. L.B. Cowman, *Streams in the Desert* (Grand Rapids, MI: Zondervan, 1997), 193; quote by Bickersteth.

Hebrews 12:11

Ezekiel 36:26

Matthew 15:13

Matthew 12:34

CHAPTER 8: THE VINEYARD

1. L.B. Cowman, *Streams in the Desert*, 249; "God has a purpose in view. Often we shrink from the purging and pruning, forgetting the Gardener knows, that the deeper the cutting and paring, the richer the luster that grows."

Romans 8:28

Genesis 41:52

Matthew 28:18-20

Isaiah 27:2-6

Isaiah 61:3

CHAPTER 9: COME FOR A SWIM

John 14:26

Song of Solomon 2:8

John 7:38

1 John 2:16

Isaiah 58:11

Jeremiah 17:8

John 16:33

Isaiah 12:3

Proverbs 18:4

Ezekiel 47:9

Isaiah 35:1

Isaiah 41:18

CHAPTER 10: WEEDS

1. Eugene H. Peterson, translator, *The Message Remix* (Carol Stream, IL: NavPress, 2011).

Isaiah 26:14

Matthew 13:25

CHAPTER 11: UNDER THE CEDAR TREE

Colossians 3:2

1 Peter 5:9

Proverbs 24:30-32

Jeremiah 17:6-7

CHAPTER 12: YOU LOOK JUST LIKE YOUR HEAVENLY FATHER

Jeremiah 18:1-6

Isaiah 45:9

Isaiah 64:8

Genesis 1:26

2 Corinthians 4:7

CHAPTER 13: I WILL CHANGE YOUR NAME

Isaiah 62:2

John 1:42

Luke 6:14

Genesis 32:24-30

Genesis 17:5, 15

Numbers 13:16

Acts 13:9

Acts 4:36

Acts 15:22

Matthew 10:13

Acts 12:25

Acts 15:37

Joel 2:25

CHAPTER 14: FRUIT

1. "It is a joy to Jesus when a person takes time to walk more intimately with Him. The bearing of fruit is always shown in Scripture to be a visible result of an intimate relationship with Jesus Christ"; *My Utmost for His Highest Journal* (January 7)

by Oswald Chambers (Uhrichsville, OH: Barbour Publishing, Inc., 2010).

John 17:3

Genesis 1:28

Galatians 5:22

John 15

Genesis 41:52

Isaiah 26:3-6

Hosea 14:8

CHAPTER 15: CROSSING THE JORDON

John 14:27

Colossians 3:15

2 Corinthians 3:6

Colossians 3:14-17

Isaiah 27:6

ACKNOWLEDGMENTS

From Emma—First and foremost, I want to thank my Beloved Jesus for walking with me in this journey to wholeness and for His precious Holy Spirit writing this with me and for me. I am eternally grateful!

I would also like to thank my husband, my next beloved (which is the meaning of my husband's name), Dave. Sometimes I am just amazed by God and how He orchestrates our lives. Thank you for encouraging me in this life as we walk it out together, and thank you for believing in me. You fill my life with laughter and are my joy. I love you so much!

To my Caleb, Abigail Murrah, you have been such an encouragement to me. Like Caleb, you looked into the Promised Land with me in many of our prayer times and said of the giants along the way, "We can take them and take this land back!" Thank you for your many prayers and for your friendship. Huge love!

To Cherri Houle and her family, I am forever grateful for your gift of prophecy and prayer for me in this journey called life. God's words, through you all, truly made me shine for Him. Thank you for your faithfulness.

To my mom, thank you for your poem written for me when I was born. Written from your heart and, I believe, from the heart of our heavenly Father, which said that I would have a love for flowers and trees. The Lord has taught me so much in these two creations of His. I love you, Mama.

To my daughter Stephani, and my sons Zackariah and Adam, and to the rest of my family and friends, thank you for your prayers, your love, and your encouragement in this journey. You are so very loved.

From Darien-- I acknowledge the role the following authors and ministries had in my life and are offered for edification in your personal Christian growth. Their materials have left obvious footprints in my life and writing for which I gratefully accredit. My devotional guides represent in many ways my own journey over the past several years.

The recommended materials are listed in the order of the ones with the longest influence to those of more recent contributions. More details and amplification of God's love and devotion will be given to you through these writings and websites. I bless you in your study and release gratitude and appreciation on those cited.

- First and foremost, I appreciate my home church—Relationship Church in Dalton, Georgia—ministry team colleagues for their support and place in my personal and spiritual growth. To Tiffany Ann Beavers, a team member, I appreciate not only the emotional support but the grammatical editing for my devotional guides. Visit www.relationshipchurch.com.

- Sylvia Gunter and Arthur Burk. *Blessing Your Spirit.* Birmingham, AL: The Father's Business, 2005. Thanks to Sylvia Gunter for permission to use her alignment of spirit, soul, and body prayer used in Devotional Guide 59. Sylvia Gunter's website: www.TheFathersBusiness.com. Arthur Burk's website: www.TheSLG.com.

- Dallas Willard. *The Divine Conspiracy: Rediscovering Our Hidden Life in God.* San Francisco: Harper, 1998.

- Dallas Willard. *Renovation of the Heart: Putting on the Character of Christ.* Colorado Springs, CO: NavPress, 2012.

- James G. Friesen, E. James Wilder, Anne M. Bierling, Rick Koepcke, Maribeth Poole. *The Life Model: Living from the Heart Jesus Gave You.* Pasadena, CA: Shepherd's House, 2004.

- E. James Wilder, Edward M. Khouri, Chris M. Coursey, Shelia D. Sutton. *Joy Starts Here: The Transformation Zone.* East Peoria, IL: Shepherd's House Inc., 2013.

- Andy Reese. *Freedom Tools for Overcoming Life's Tough Problems*. Grand Rapids, MI: Chosen Books, 2008 www.thefreedomresource.org.

- Karl Lehman. *Outsmarting Yourself: Catching Your Past Invading the Present and What to Do About It*. Libertyville, IL: This Joy! Books, 2011. Website: www.KCLehman.com.

- Andrew Miller. Healing the Broken Hearted Seminars. Andrew Miller's website: www.heartsyncministries.org/what-is-heartsync.html. Also Dr. Tom and Diane W. Hawkins's website is a wonderful resource: www.rcm-usa.org.

- David Takle. *Forming: Change by Grace*. Pasadena, CA: Shepherd's House, 2011.

- Chester and Betsy Kylstra. *Restoring the Foundations*. Hendersonville, NC: Proclaiming His Word Publications, 2001. This book greatly influenced some of the appendixes.

- Kelley Varner. *Chosen for Greatness: Discover Your Personal Destiny*. Shippensburg, PA: Destiny Image, 2003. This book inspired Devotional Guide 3 tremendously, to which I gladly give credit.

- Liberty Savard. *The Unsurrendered Soul*. Orlando, FL: Bridge-Logos, 2002. Devotional Guide 57 was inspired by Liberty Savard's books, to which I gladly give credit.

- Harold R Eberle. *Grace: The Power to Reign*. Yakima, WA: Worldcast Publishing, 2001.

- Clark Whitten. *Pure Grace: The Life Changing Power of Uncontaminated Grace*. Shippensburg, PA: Destiny Image Publishers, 2012.

- Thom Gardner. *Relentless Love: Unfolding God's Passion, Presence, and Glory*. Shippensburg, PA: Destiny Image Publishers, 2012.

- Henry Cloud and John Townsend. *Boundaries: When to Say Yes, How to Say No to Take Control of Your Life.* Grand Rapids, MI: Zondervan Publishing House, 1992.

- Juanita Ryan. "Recovery from Childhood Trauma" (June 16, 2008) is an article I have recently discovered, read, and gleaned truths; www.nacr.org/wordpress/37/recovery-from-childhood-abuse; accessed November 24, 2014.

ABOUT THE AUTHORS

Emma Kelln is the founder of Garden Within Ministries. Her heart's greatest desire is for you to walk in the destiny that God planned for you before you were ever born. She teaches a twelve-week course called The Garden Within: A Journey to Wholeness, where her participants experience this journey and have a chance to spend time with Jesus, the lover of their souls, in the secret place. She lives in Loveland, Colorado, with her husband, Dave. They have five children and eight grandchildren. Contact Emma Kelln at www.gradenwithinministries.com.

Darien B. Cooper is a wife, mother, lecturer, and author of eight books including the best-seller, *You Can Be the Wife of a Happy Husband*, with more than one million in print, as well as a Gold Medallion finalist. Her practical teaching on marriage and complete abandonment to Jesus Christ has changed countless lives both in the USA and abroad. After graduating from Carson-Newman College in Jefferson City, Tennessee, with a degree in Sociology and Psychology, she and her husband, DeWitt, served as associate staff with Campus Crusade for Christ Lay Ministry in the early 1970s. Then in the mid-1980s they served as missionaries with Family Consultation Service, a ministry to the poor in the inner city of Atlanta, Georgia, for eight years. In 1993 they left Atlanta, their home for 35 years, to move to North Georgia. Darien and DeWitt have three sons and three daughters-in-love who have given them an international family with five of their twelve grandchildren having been adopted from three other nationalities. Contact Darien B. Cooper at www.darienbcooper.com.

Made in the USA
San Bernardino, CA
29 January 2016